EPIC IMPACT™

TRANSFORM YOUR MESSAGE
INTO A MOVEMENT

HAILEY EVANS

This book is dedicated to:

Every mission-driven leader who has ever felt the gap between their impact and their ability to communicate it. You're the nonprofit directors writing grant proposals at midnight, the entrepreneurs struggling to explain why their work matters, the coaches who change lives but can't capture it in words, and the changemakers who know their message could spark a movement—if only they could find the right way to share it.

This is for those who refuse to let messaging struggles overshadow their mission, who are ready to bridge the gap between their results and their results and influence.

You are just one story away…

EPIC IMPACT™: TRANSFORM YOUR MESSAGE INTO A MOVEMENT

CAPTIVATE SUPPORTERS. INSPIRE ACTION. LEAD WITH STORY + AI.

The proven framework for transforming messages into movements, now enhanced by intelligent technology.

CONTENTS

PRAISE FOR EPIC IMPACT™

"Your story isn't connecting because you're telling it the wrong way. Hailey Evans has created a storytelling framework that's not only clear and flexible but also scalable. If you're in fundraising, sales, or any role where storytelling drives action, this book shows you exactly how to make it work. It combines powerful story structure with AI-driven workflows in a way that's both practical and effective. I've had the privilege of previewing many books. Most are good. Some are great.

This one? I'd be tempted to steal from it—if Hailey hadn't already handed us the entire blueprint."

—Holland Webb, Editor

PART 1: YOU DON'T NEED MORE TOOLS. YOU NEED BETTER STRATEGY.

REFRAME THE WAY YOU THINK ABOUT STORY, CLARITY, AND CONNECTION.

CHAPTER 1: ONE STORY AWAY®

WHY THE STORY YOU'RE AFRAID TO TELL IS THE ONE THAT COULD SET YOU FREE.

Chapter 1: One Story Away®

I clutched a clipboard with trembling hands in the Department of Social Services waiting room. The overhead lights buzzed and flickered, as if they hadn't worked properly in years. Toddlers wailed. A woman beside me whispered a prayer in Spanish, her voice barely audible above the chaos.

I wasn't supposed to be here.

Just months earlier, I had been the soccer mom who never missed a game, the devoted wife planning anniversary trips, the Bible study leader with all the right answers for other women's struggles. Now I couldn't answer how I'd feed my own children next week.

I had been a devoted mother who packed lunches with handwritten notes, kissed scraped knees, and read bedtime stories in character voices. I mentored women through late-night phone calls, quietly becoming a pillar in my community. I led with compassion, gave without hesitation, and showed up for everyone. Now, I was the one needing help, and so far, nobody was showing up for me. Aside from some financial help from my parents who were doing their best with what they had, I felt utterly alone.

What brought me to that cracked vinyl chair wasn't circumstance but the complete unraveling of everything I thought defined me. A marriage destroyed by betrayal. Financial security vanished overnight. The future I had carefully planned, gone.

I was 31. No degree. No savings. No plan. Only the hope that I could somehow rebuild from the wreckage.

I thought I was finished.

But I was just getting started.

What changed everything? A story.

Not just any story, but a structured story that would eventually become the framework I'm about to share with you.

The Humiliation I Wasn't Prepared For

Instead of my sons coming home to me after school, I was now watching the neighbor's children to make ends meet. The guilt was suffocating, as I chose between being present for my own boys and earning just enough to keep the lights on.

The worst part? Through the neighbor's window, I could see my front yard where my boys practiced soccer alone. Some days it felt like watching my life through glass, caring for someone else's children while mine waited for me to come home.

Then came the scholarship application for my son's soccer club.

My fingers hovered over the keyboard at the question: "Why do you need financial assistance?"

What I wanted to type: "My jackass husband decided to live a double life and I was the last to find out."

What I actually wrote: "Our family is in need."

Five words to summarize the complete obliteration of our former life.

But inside my head, the real conversation raged: "God, am I really that stupid? How did I miss all the signs? How could he look into my eyes every day, tell me how blessed he was, brag to friends about his perfect family, while living a lie?"

The Story That Tried to Break Me—And How I Took the Pen Back

After my divorce, the boys and I lived off food stamps and Medicaid. I juggled side jobs, babysitting, flipping thrift store finds on eBay, anything to survive. Every night, I tucked my sons into bed with whispered prayers and promises I wasn't sure I could keep.

I knew education was my only way out of the black hole threatening to swallow us whole. I'd missed my chance the first time around, graduating high school a year early, only to discover I was pregnant three weeks before graduation. The weight of disappointing my highly educated, accomplished parents crushed me.

As their only child, I'd carried their dreams alongside my own, and suddenly both seemed impossible. But now, years later, I understood that education served a deeper purpose than fulfilling their expectations. If I didn't fight for a future, this cycle would repeat forever.

I quickly completed my associate's degree and landed my first job, a start, but I knew it wasn't enough. To make a real difference in our long-term sustainability, I needed to continue pursuing my bachelor's and eventually my master's degree. That's why this next opportunity mattered so much.

Then one night, after the boys were asleep, I picked up a pen. Not to vent. Not to journal. But to tell the truth, on paper.

A Women's Leadership Foundation scholarship had opened up. I'd made it through the first round. Now they wanted an in-person interview eight hours away. No Zoom. No exceptions.

And I had exactly zero paid time off left at my low-wage job. My boss was already frustrated with my frequent absences, court dates, doctor's visits, and the messy reality of rebuilding a broken life. Never mind that I had no family in the area to help me with the boys. One more absence could cost me the only steady income I had.

I couldn't afford to lose my job. But I also couldn't pass up this opportunity.

Eight Hours to Everything or Nothing

Eight hours of interstate stretched ahead of me, every mile heavy with self-doubt. The radio crackled with static, broken signals searching for something clear to hold onto. My hands gripped the steering wheel until my knuckles went white. What if I'm not enough? What if they see right through me?

This scholarship was my lifeline. Without it, I'd be trapped in the cycle of low-wage jobs forever, unable to afford the education I needed to build real security for my boys. This was my shot at breaking free from food stamps and midnight side hustles, my chance to show my sons that we could rise above what happened to us.

I walked into that conference room clutching a three-ring binder, literally the only proof I had that I deserved to be there.

Five accomplished women sat across a polished mahogany table, their eyes kind but unreadable. The air conditioning hummed. Someone's pen clicked against the table.

My hands trembled as I opened that binder.

I didn't hand them a polished resume. I didn't pitch perfection.

I told my story.

Raw. Unfiltered. Everything.

I brought them into my world: the shame of relying on food stamps when my $15-an-hour job didn't cover monthly expenses. The desperation of babysitting other people's children at night while my own boys did homework alone. The terror of racing to my son's doctor appointments after his fourth concussion from soccer, wondering if this time the damage would be permanent.

I spoke of empty fridges and late-night essays, of hospital visits and hallway breakdowns, of court dates followed by sideline cheers at soccer games. The stress had worn me down to a frail 93 pounds, leaving me so exhausted that weekends were spent bedridden, gathering strength just to face another week. I shared how I was fighting not just for a scholarship, but for a future I refused to surrender.

But I didn't stop there. I painted them a picture of the woman I was determined to become, not just for me, but for my sons, who were watching their mother either crumble or rise.

What I didn't realize then was that I was telling a powerful story. I was instinctively using what would later become the **EPIC Framework™**, *engaging* those women with authentic struggles, *persuading* with concrete details, *inspiring* with vision, and *closing* with absolute clarity about what I needed.

As they listened, their faces changed. They leaned forward. They were with me. At least, I thought they were.

But the week that followed was pure agony.

Was it enough? *Was I enough?*

The Phone Call

A week later, my phone rang.

"Congratulations," the voice said. "You got it."

That $5,000 scholarship brought more than money; it gave me permission to believe I could rebuild.

One single story became the key to securing a total of $52,000 in scholarships and grants. In five years, I earned three degrees, including my MBA, while working full-time and raising my boys.

That story and the education it made possible opened doors to stages, leadership opportunities at major women's events, and a future I thought I'd lost forever. I was even selected to speak on behalf of all 400 scholarship recipients for the university's office of philanthropy.

More importantly, telling my story taught me that words, true words, can move mountains.

What Stories Like Mine Unlock

You might think your stories are too small, too ordinary, or too unfinished. But what moves people to give, volunteer, and stay engaged isn't perfection but humanity.

The world doesn't need more polished marketing. It needs real moments. Real people. Real impact.

I've seen this principle transform organizations beyond my personal journey. When Covenant House, a nonprofit serving homeless youth, shifted from statistics-heavy appeals to structured storytelling, their results were staggering. Instead of program metrics, they shared Kevin's story, a teenager who fled an abusive home and found safety at Covenant House. The moment that changed everything for him? Receiving his GED and saying, "This is the first time I felt like my future could be different than my past."

When Covenant House restructured their appeals using this story-centered approach, their donor response rates increased by 36% and average gift size grew by 42% compared to their previous statistics-focused appeals.

Why? Because someone out there is sitting in their own version of a cracked vinyl chair, questioning whether their gift would matter. Wondering if anyone sees their time, their heart, their sacrifice. Hoping their story counts for something.

They don't need another flyer. They need a reason to believe.

And they sure as hell don't need more stats and facts. What they do need is a story that makes them feel something. A story that makes them care.

Your stories can be that reason.

The Framework Behind Every Movement

Over the next chapters, I'll teach you the exact framework that turned my rock bottom into rocket fuel: EPIC.

E - Engage their attention with an opening that connects instantly and earns the right to be heard.

P - Persuade with a story and proof that transforms information into feeling.

I - Inspire a bigger vision that elevates identity beyond simple action.

C - Close with clarity that makes the next step inevitable, not optional.

EPIC goes beyond a formula for writing content. It's a structure that transforms messages into movements.

You are just one story away from breakthrough.

Want to see the full power of storytelling in action? Visit haileyevans.com/onestoryaway (or scan the QR code below) to watch a 3-minute video of my complete story from that scholarship committee room to where I am today.

This book is the 'why' and the resources are the 'strategy.'

Visit **epicimpact.com** or scan the QR code to download your free **EPIC Impact™ Starter Kit** so you can access all the templates, worksheets, and resources mentioned throughout this book.

Let's begin.

Coming up in Chapter 2: Why the loudest voices in the room are often the least effective, and the one word that changes everything.

i

CHAPTER 2: NOISE ISN'T THE ENEMY, CONFUSION IS

YOU DON'T NEED TO SCREAM LOUDER. YOU NEED TO SPEAK CLEARER.

"People visit our donation page," the marketing director told me, "but they almost never give. Why?" The problem wasn't disinterest but confusion.

Most of us have been taught that getting attention means making more noise than everyone else. Marketing gurus, fundraising experts, and social media managers all seem to preach the same message. Be louder, post more content, send yet another donor appeal email. But the most effective communicators understand something different.

Our world is cluttered with noise. Clarity is a quiet rebellion.

Real communicators choose precision over pandemonium. Because they know confusion comes with a price - lost support, broken trust, wasted time. Clarity, on the other hand, is the shortest path to connection. It cuts through noise like nothing else can. Choose clarity.

Drowning in Communication Overload

Inbox overload. That's what most donors face. Not disinterest. Not stinginess. Just too much noise.

Every nonprofit is sitting on a goldmine of stories. How can you gather and communicate those stories in a compelling way that moves people to act? It all starts with asking the right questions to get the story that can move the needle. Most organizations skip this crucial first step and focus only on the outcome.

Greenville Technical College Foundation could tell powerful stories of student transformation. But instead, their donor communications were scattered, generic emails that buried compelling stories beneath unclear messaging.

Before the Foundation clarified their message, donors opened emails but rarely responded. The result? Low engagement. Passive donors. Few replies.

Not because people didn't care. But because people didn't understand why they should give.

Structure Over Shouting

During one consulting session with Ann Wright, VP of Advancement at Greenville Technical College Foundation, I casually suggested an idea.

"What if you created something called 'Transformation Tuesday'?" I offered. "Every week, share just one student story, one journey of change."

It was a simple suggestion during a broader conversation about donor communications. I didn't think much would come of it. But six months later, Ann called with surprising news.

They had indeed launched the strategy. Every Tuesday, a new story went out to donors. One student. One turning point. One emotionally resonant message. One clear call to action.

This relentless focus was the difference.

No data dumps. No program updates. No mission statements. Just stories structured with precision.

By applying the four pillars of the **EPIC Framework™**, the foundation transformed generic asks into stories that moved people to take action. Instead of starting with 'Please donate to help our students,' they began with stories like "She kept her textbooks in her car, not because she was disorganized, but because she was homeless."

When the Greenville Tech Foundation started using strategic questions to gather student stories (we'll cover the exact question framework in Chapter 13), they stopped getting responses like "The scholarship helped me" and started hearing stories like "I kept my textbooks in my car because I was homeless, but this scholarship didn't just pay for school—it gave me hope that I could break the cycle for my daughters."

After implementing "Transformation Tuesday," the foundation's inbox filled with replies asking, "How can I help?" The clarity in their message created immediate momentum.

Results After Six Months: Open Rates Doubled and Click Rates More Than Doubled

Metric	Previous Annual Average	After 6 Months	Change
Open Rate	22.8%	45.1%	97.81% increase
Click Rate	0.4%	0.87%	117.5% increase

Suddenly, donors weren't just reading, they were responding. Staff members were proud to share. Board members forwarded the emails. Stories became momentum.

The only thing that changed? The clarity of the message.

After I used the **EPIC Framework™** to write a story about one of Greenville Tech's beloved students, Ann shared, *"We received an email immediately from a CEO of a company that I had been trying to reach for six months! He read your story and wants to donate to The Foundation."*

That's the power of clear storytelling. It does more than improve metrics; it opens doors that seemed permanently closed.

The Case for Clarity

Clarity is good communication and a moral act. It allows people to make informed decisions, feel empowered, and confidently say yes to something that aligns with their values.

Think about it. If someone doesn't fully understand what you do, how you help, or why it matters... They can't donate. They can't join. They can't act.

And that's not just a missed opportunity. It's a breach of trust.

You've got a clarity problem.

One of the fastest ways to test your clarity? Ask someone else to explain what you do.

If they say something like "They do something with families, I think?" "It's kind of like education, but also mental health?" "They help people... somehow?"

You've got a clarity problem.

Here's the thing. You are too close to your message. You're immersed in the details. You know all the moving parts, programs, outcomes, and nuances. But your audience doesn't.

It's what I call the "bottle effect." You can't see the label from inside.

They need a simplified version of your core message, something short enough to repeat and strong enough to remember.

And they need it fast.

Confusion breeds hesitation. Clarity creates momentum.

In the nonprofit world, we're often taught to focus on inspiration. Emotion. Passion. And yes, those things matter. But inspiration without understanding is like a match without fuel. It might spark, but it won't last.

When you bring clarity to your messaging, you do three powerful things. You respect your audience's time and cognitive energy. You equip people to advocate on your behalf. You make it easy to take the next step.

Clarity isn't a marketing tactic. It's a leadership responsibility.

The Brain Loves Simple

There's a reason clarity is so powerful. It literally aligns with how our brains work.

Cognitive science tells us that the brain is a "cognitive miser" - it conserves energy by avoiding unnecessary mental work. So when people encounter a message that's long-winded, complex, or abstract, their brains instinctively disengage.

In other words, if your message takes too long to process, your audience won't try.

That's not rudeness. That's biology.

Clarity is how you earn someone's attention. It's how you show respect. It's how you remove barriers between intention and action.

As Brené Brown writes in *Dare to Lead*, "Clear is kind. Unclear is unkind."

What Makes a Story Great?

Each time I lead a workshop, I open with a simple question, "What makes for a great story?"

I get answers like:

• A strong character

• Authenticity

• A good plot

• Emotion

• A satisfying ending

- Connection

- Vulnerability

- A clear journey from beginning to end

- Maybe even a little tension or surprise

Then I take it one step further, "What's one word you'd use to describe exceptional communication?"

People call out words like:

- Passionate

- Compelling

- Inspiring

- Memorable

- Bold

- Relatable

- Strategic

But in all my years of doing this, no one has ever said the one word that matters most. **Clarity.**

And yet, the moment I say it, heads nod. You can see the realization land.

Why is clarity so rarely top of mind? *Because we assume people will work hard to understand us.* They won't. Not because they don't care, but because they're exhausted.

If donors are confused, they can't say yes. If volunteers are unsure of what you need, they won't show up. If staff or board members are unclear on the vision, they won't champion it. If your story is emotionally vague or structurally scattered, it won't stick.

Before you continue reading, pause and ask yourself:

• What was the last story that truly moved you to action?

• What specific element made it impossible to ignore?

• Did it give you absolute clarity about what to do next?

Why Specific Details Matter

Let's go deeper. One of the most common messaging mistakes I see? Vagueness.

We say things like "We help people in need." "We offer personalized service." "We create impact."

But vague language doesn't stick. Specificity is what makes a message memorable.

Look at these upgraded examples:

Vague	Specific
"We help veterans transition."	"We provide 6-month welding certifications, transitional housing for up to 18 months, and mentor matching for 85 veterans annually."
"We make a difference."	"We've helped over 300 single moms secure jobs and stable housing in 12 months."
"We create beautiful spaces."	"We turn empty lots into thriving gardens with composting workshops and free produce stands for families in food deserts."

Details build trust. They paint a picture in the listener's mind. They eliminate ambiguity and fuel belief.

Clear Messages Change Lives

Clarity isn't just kind. It's effective. It's ethical. It's essential.

Because when people understand what you do and why it matters, they lean in.

Want to know if your message is working?

Three Ways to Test Your Message Clarity Today:

1 The 12-Year-Old Test - Explain your mission to a middle-schooler. If they can't repeat it back accurately, simplify until they can.

2 The Stranger Exercise - Ask someone who's never heard of your work to read your homepage or fundraising letter. Then ask them to explain what you do and why it matters. Note where they hesitate or get confused.

3 The Seven-Second Scan - Time how long it takes someone to understand what you're asking them to do in your email or social post. If it's over seven seconds, your call to action needs clarification.

Is Your Online Message Clear in 7 Seconds?

Take a quick audit of your homepage. Your header should instantly answer three questions:

1 What's your mission? (Who you serve and what problem you solve)

2 How does it change lives? (The transformation or impact)

3 How can someone get involved? (Donate, volunteer, join, etc.)

*(For deeper website strategy, **visit haileyevans.com/training** or scan the QR code, including why putting social media icons in your header may be quietly killing your conversions.)*

Clarity creates connection, and structure is how you get clarity. If your message isn't clear, it's not compelling. If it's not compelling, people won't act. Your audience isn't distracted. They're just waiting for a message that cuts through the noise.

Coming up in Chapter 3: The most expensive lie nonprofit communicators believe and why giving people more information actually makes them less likely to donate.

i

CHAPTER 3: CLARITY IS KINDNESS (AND POWER)

IF PEOPLE DON'T UNDERSTAND YOU, THEY CAN'T SAY YES.

The most expensive lie nonprofit communicators believe is this: Giving supporters more information means they'll give us more money.

We often think more data, more statistics, and more program details will drive donations.

But research and case studies show the opposite is true.

Consider the case of Duffy Health Foundation. When they simplified their annual appeal letter from three pages of program descriptions to a single page focused on one patient's story, their response rate increased by 28% compared to the previous year.

This pattern repeats across organizations of all sizes: clarity outperforms complexity every time. The point isn't about saying less. It's about being understood. We don't need more content; we need more connection. Every sentence must carry the weight of our purpose, and none of it should feel like work to read.

Clarity as a Leadership Tool

Let's take it further.

Clarity goes beyond communication; it's a leadership trait.

When leaders speak clearly, teams align faster. When organizations write clearly, supporters engage more. When causes share clear stories, movements grow.

But when clarity is missing? Volunteers get confused. Staff members waste time. Board members tune out. Contributors hesitate or disappear.

If you're seeing confusion inside or outside your organization, ask yourself, "Have I made it clear what matters most?"

Clarity transforms every aspect of leadership:

Performance Feedback - Clear feedback eliminates guesswork. Instead of "You need to improve your donor outreach," try "Your last three donor emails had subject lines that didn't mention the impact. Next week, write subject lines that lead with transformation, like 'Sarah's scholarship changed everything.'" Specific, actionable feedback accelerates growth.

Recruiting Top Talent - High performers are drawn to clarity. They want to know exactly what success looks like, how their role creates impact, and what growth opportunities exist. When job descriptions clearly outline expectations and outcomes, you attract candidates who thrive on clear direction rather than those who need constant clarification.

Delegation and Accountability - Clear instructions prevent rework and frustration. "Handle the volunteer appreciation event" becomes "Plan a 90-minute volunteer appreciation dinner for 50 people on March 15th, with testimonials from three clients and a clear ask for continued commitment." Your team delivers what you actually need.

Strategic Planning - Clear vision statements unite teams around common goals. Vague missions like "serve the community" become "provide job training and placement services that help 200 unemployed adults secure stable employment within six months." Everyone knows exactly what success means.

Conflict Resolution - Clarity cuts through workplace tension. Instead of letting issues fester, address them directly. "I've noticed tension in team meetings. Let's discuss what's working and what isn't so we can move forward effectively." Clear conversation prevents small problems from becoming organizational crises.

The most effective leaders use clarity as their primary tool for building trust, accelerating results, and creating the kind of workplace culture that attracts and retains exceptional people.

Why Clarity Drives Growth: Real-World Case Studies

Research consistently demonstrates that clarity directly affects engagement and results. Here is an example from published studies and documented case histories:

Case Study: Oklahoma Medical Research Foundation
When OMRF simplified their communications: Email response rates increased by over 30% Average gift size grew by 17% Long-term supporter retention improved by 24%

This illustrates a consistent pattern: organizations that prioritize clarity in their messaging consistently outperform those that rely on complexity. The evidence is clear—simplicity works.

When your message is clear, people don't just understand you. They believe you. They trust you. They act.

Clarity Checklist: Is Your Message Working?

Let's make this practical. Use this checklist to evaluate your current message:

☐ **Can someone outside your organization repeat what you do in one sentence?**

☐ **Is the transformation you offer crystal clear?**

☐ **Have you removed jargon, acronyms, or insider language?**

☐ **Is your language specific and emotionally resonant?**

If you answered "no" to even one of these, it's time for a clarity tune-up.

For a complete checklist with a scoring guide and real-world examples of before-and-after message transformations, refer to the **EPIC Impact™ Starter Kit** (linked in Chapter 3).

Quick Exercise: Score Your Message

Grab your organization's **mission statement, a recent email, or your website homepage**, and score each of the four questions above on a scale of 1–5:

• **1** = Needs serious improvement

• **3** = Adequate but could be better

• **5** = Excellent

Add up your points.

What your total score means:

• **20–25:** Strong message—well done!

• **15–19:** Room for improvement—some clarity opportunities.

Below 15: Significant clarity gaps—time to refocus and refine.

Question	Score
Does your audience immediately understand what you do?	———
Is the message emotionally engaging?	———
Does it inspire action?	———
Is the language clear and jargon-free?	———
Is the story consistent with your brand?	———
Total	———

You Don't Need Fancy Words. You Need the Right Ones.

Formality often creates distance.

We sometimes hide behind complexity because it feels more "professional." But authenticity, specificity, and clarity connect far more deeply than polish ever will.

You don't need to impress people. You need to move them.

That means telling the truth clearly. Making the ask directly. And removing every barrier between your story and your audience's heart.

From Misunderstood to Magnetic

Let's circle back to the original idea: If people don't understand you, they can't say yes.

Clarity doesn't just help you stand out. It helps you get chosen.

When funders, volunteers, or partners understand exactly what you do and why it matters, you don't have to beg. You don't have to over-explain. You don't have to overcompensate.

You simply invite them into a story they already believe in.

And that is the true power of clarity.

Clarity in Action: The EPIC Intro

Want a real-world test of clarity? Try this:

The next time someone asks you, "What do you do?" pay attention to how long it takes you to answer.

If it takes longer than 7 seconds, you've likely lost them.

In all my years as a coach, strategist, and trainer, nothing has been more profound or more transformational than helping leaders get this one thing right: their EPIC Intro.

Because when a leader can clearly articulate who they help, how they help, and the transformation they create, everything changes. Engagement deepens. Confidence grows. Supporters lean in. Teams rally.

That's why I commit to every workshop with one promise: every leader will walk away with a message that's clear, compelling, and easy to remember, something tangible they can repeat with confidence and use to inspire action immediately.

To help you get there, we use the EPIC Intro, a powerful, three-part statement that reflects the core of your mission. It's short. It's specific. And it mirrors the proven structure of the EPIC Framework:

The EPIC Intro Formula:

Start with the Problem (Engage): Capture attention by naming a challenge your audience recognizes and cares about. Explain Your Solution (Persuade): Build connection by sharing your specific approach or offering. End with the Outcome (Inspire): Elevate the vision by showing the transformation your work creates.

The Close happens in how you deliver it, with confidence, clarity, and an invitation to continue the conversation.

Why It Works

It follows the natural storytelling pattern that the brain is wired to process. It places your audience (not your organization) at the center of the story. It focuses on transformation, not just information.

You don't need just one version either. The versatility of the EPIC Intro allows you to customize your message for different audiences and purposes:

Examples of EPIC Intros for Different Purposes

Donor-Focused Intro: Many teens in foster care age out without a safety net. (Engage with a problem supporters care about) We provide life skills training, mentorship, and housing support. (Persuade with your specific solution) So they can transition into adulthood with confidence and community. (Inspire with the transformation)

Volunteer-Focused Intro: Thousands of adults in our city struggle to read. (Engage potential volunteers with the need) We train volunteers to tutor them one-on-one. (Persuade with how they specifically fit in) So they can build independence, get better jobs, and change their future. (Inspire with the impact volunteers create)

Organization Mission Intro: Every day, tons of food go to waste while families go hungry. (Engage with the problem) We connect restaurants and grocers to local food banks. (Persuade with your unique approach) So good food feeds people, not landfills. (Inspire with the dual outcome)

Capital Campaign Intro: Our current facility limits how many children we can serve each day. (Engage with the constraint) We're building a new youth center with double the capacity and modern resources. (Persuade with the specific project) So no child has to wait for the mentorship and educational support they need today. (Inspire with the vision)

Your Turn: Create Your EPIC Intro

Take 10 minutes to write 2–3 EPIC Intros for your organization or business. Try one for each audience you serve (clients, funders, volunteers, teams).

Step 1: Draft your problem statement (Engage) - What challenge does your audience recognize and care about? Step 2: Craft your solution statement (Persuade) - How do you specifically address this challenge? Step 3: Write your outcome statement (Inspire) - What transformation results from your work?

Say it out loud. If someone can't easily repeat it back to you or if their eyes glaze over, simplify it.

Because when people understand what you do through this EPIC structure, they're far more likely to say yes to being part of it.

Real-World Success: The EPIC Intro in Action

I recently had the pleasure of meeting Michaela Salinas at a Leadership Luncheon I led. Two weeks later, we met for lunch, and within an hour, it felt like we had been friends for years. Michaela's deep passion for the American Heart Association was clear as she shared how her father's struggle with heart disease has fueled her mission to support ongoing research and provide solutions for those battling the condition daily.

Here's what Michaela had to say about mastering her EPIC Intro:

*"Hailey Evans' EPIC Intro Workshop beautifully illustrated the power of storytelling in crafting effective messages. Using the **EPIC Framework™**, Hailey guided us through identifying challenges, showcasing solutions, and articulating the impact of our work—all while making our message clearer and more intentional for the people we serve. Her easy, step-by-step process made creating my EPIC Intro simple, while also serving as a powerful reminder of how storytelling drives deeper emotional connections with our supporters."*

— Michaela Salinas, Director of Development at American Heart Association

And here's Michaela's EPIC Intro in action:

"Cardiovascular disease is the leading cause of death, but change starts within our community. The Upstate Heart Walk is dedicated to turning bystanders into lifesavers by ensuring every participant learns hands-only CPR, empowering our community to save lives in cardiac emergencies."

Notice how Michaela's EPIC Intro follows the framework perfectly:

• **Engage:** "Cardiovascular disease is the leading cause of death" (problem everyone recognizes)

• **Persuade:** "The Upstate Heart Walk is dedicated to turning bystanders into lifesavers" (specific solution)

• **Inspire:** "Empowering our community to save lives in cardiac emergencies" (transformation and bigger vision)

. . .

This is the power of clarity in action. When your message is structured and clear, it doesn't just inform—it transforms. It turns strangers into friends, supporters into champions, and messages into movements.

Michaela's EPIC Intro does more than explain what the Heart Walk does. It creates urgency, builds confidence, and invites participation in something bigger than a single event. That's what happens when clarity meets purpose.

Your turn to create that same impact starts now.

—

Coming up in Chapter 4: Why your perfectly researched presentations are instantly forgettable and the one scientific discovery that explains why stories are 22 times more powerful than facts.

Ready to craft your perfect EPIC Intro? Visit **epicimpact.com** or scan the QR code for the complete EPIC Intro worksheet and additional examples that will help you find the exact words that capture your mission.

CHAPTER 4: WHAT MAKES A MESSAGE STICK?

WHY STORIES ARE 22X MORE MEMORABLE

What Neuroscience Reveals and Why Stories Beat Stats

According to cognitive psychologist Jerome Bruner, we are 22 times more likely to remember a fact when it's wrapped in a story than when it's presented as a standalone data point (Actual Minds, Possible Worlds, 1986).

That's not fluff. That's how the brain retains meaning.

Because story gives the brain what it craves:

• A relatable character

• Emotional stakes

• A problem to solve

• Specific Details

• A satisfying resolution

. . .

From Confusion to Forgettable Let me give you a real-world example.

Last month, I spoke to a council of nonprofit leaders and brought a stack of donor letters with me. I pulled out one and started reading it aloud.

It was filled with important facts, statistics, and formal language.

Halfway through, people started laughing.

I paused and asked, "What's funny?"

One woman shrugged and said, "We already forgot what you just said."

Exactly.

The letter was informative but completely forgettable. It read like something pulled from the pages of Wikipedia. No story. No emotion. No reason to care.

So I took out my phone, snapped a photo of the letter, and ran it through my **EPIC Framework™** using ChatGPT.

Five-point-six seconds later, I had a new version. It still included the facts, but now it had heart, structure, and clarity, too.

I read the revised version out loud.

This time? Eyes widened. Heads nodded. One person whispered, "Now that I'd actually respond to."

It wasn't about being louder or more dramatic.

It was about clarity with a story that stuck.

Here is the intro before and after BEFORE version (data-driven and generic):

Every night, over 3,000 individuals in South Carolina are homeless. Veterans are especially vulnerable. Our organization is launching a campaign to expand services.

Technically accurate but emotionally flat.

Here's the AFTER version, rewritten using storytelling:

Ethan's story began with heartbreak but ended with hope. For years, he struggled with addiction and broken relationships. At our organization, he didn't just find shelter: he rebuilt his life, paid off debts, and spent Christmas reconciled with his father. "For the first time, I felt whole," he said.

Same campaign. Radically different emotional impact.

The first version may be informative, but the second is unforgettable.

Because people don't respond to stats. They respond to stories.

The Neuroscience Behind Sticky Messages If your message isn't landing, it's not a lack of intelligence, it's a lack of alignment with the brain's natural preferences.

Here's how stories activate the brain in powerful, science-backed ways:

Mirror Neurons: When someone hears a story, their brain activates as if they are experiencing the story themselves. Mirror neurons, discovered in the 1990s, create this empathy and emotional connection (Rizzolatti & Craighero, 2004).

EPIC Connection: This is why the Engage component of The **EPIC Framework™** starts with a relatable character or situation to immediately activate mirror neurons and create connection.

Oxytocin Release: Emotionally compelling stories trigger oxytocin (the "trust hormone"), which increases empathy and bonding between storyteller and listener. This makes people more generous, trusting, and open to action (Zak, 2013, Why Inspiring Stories Make Us React).

EPIC Connection: The Persuade element works because emotional details in your story literally change your audience's biochemistry, making them more receptive to your message.

Narrative Transportation: When people become immersed in a story, they experience narrative transportation, a state in which they are less critical, more trusting, and more likely to be persuaded (Green & Brock, 2000).

EPIC Connection: The Inspire component leverages narrative transportation to help people envision a better future and connect to a larger purpose.

Cognitive Ease: The brain is a "cognitive miser" that avoids effort wherever possible (Fiske & Taylor, 1991). When information is too complex, the brain tunes out. But when it's organized in a familiar narrative format, it flows effortlessly.

EPIC Connection: The Close element provides absolute clarity about next steps, reducing cognitive load and making action inevitable, not optional.

How Story Changes Everything: Evidence-Based Results Multiple research projects have documented the impact of story-based messaging on audience engagement and response. According to research compiled in "The Science of Giving" (Oppenheimer & Olivola, 2011), organizations that implement structured storytelling consistently see measurable improvements in multiple metrics:

Small Contributor Communications Research by the Donor Voice (2018): Small nonprofits using story-centered supporter communications saw open rates increase from an average of 17% to 31% over a six-month period.

Higher Education Advancement by Sargeant and Shang (2017): University foundations using beneficiary storytelling in their appeals received average donations 40% higher than those in control groups receiving traditional institutional appeals.

Healthcare Fundraising by the Center on Philanthropy (2019): A controlled analysis found that healthcare organizations using patient stories in their communications secured 2.5 times more corporate partnerships than those using primarily statistics-based appeals.

Cultural Institution Engagement Research published in the Journal of Arts Management (Lee & Skadberg, 2020): Museums using story-centered volunteer recruitment saw retention rates four times higher than those using primarily opportunity-based recruitment.

These research findings demonstrate a consistent pattern: story-based messaging produces significantly stronger results across multiple sectors and metrics than traditional information-centered approaches.

Why Can't People Remember Your Bullet Points? You've probably seen it happen.

You deliver a well-researched, carefully crafted presentation with stats, slides, and sound logic.

But days later, what do people remember?

Not the numbers. Not the data points. Maybe not even your name.

What sticks is the story.

"Where do unexpected donations come from?"

This question surfaces regularly in nonprofit discussions when organizations experience unexpected fundraising success. Communication research consistently reveals the same pattern: Story-driven messages consistently outperform statistic-heavy ones.

The Network for Good Digital Giving Index (2021) documented multiple cases where nonprofits saw significant donation increases after shifting from program descriptions to story-focused appeals. In one notable example, a veterans' organization saw a 26% increase in response rate after reformatting their communications to lead with a beneficiary story rather than organizational accomplishments.

As fundraising expert Tom Ahern explains in "How to Write Fundraising Materials that Raise More Money" (2016): "People don't give to organizations. They give through organizations to help people."

This insight explains why story-centered communications consistently outperform data-centered ones because what moves people isn't information, but transformation.

Story as a Shortcut to Belief In a world overwhelmed with content and skepticism, story becomes the shortcut.

It speeds up trust. It bypasses resistance. It builds belief.

That's why some organizations struggle to get attention, while others capture hearts with a single post, video, or donor appeal.

When you use story, you multiply your reach and your resonance.

Why This Matters for Mission-Driven Leaders Whether you're pitching a board, writing a grant, launching a campaign, or speaking at an event, your audience craves clarity, but they commit through emotion.

This is why:

- Supporters give to people, not programs.
- Volunteers serve when they feel connected.
- Sponsors sign on when they trust the mission.
- And all of that happens faster through storytelling.

The Story-Driven Litmus Test Ask yourself:

□ **Can I name one person in this story?**

□ **Is there a clear before-and-after transformation?**

□ **Does the story evoke genuine emotion?**

□ **Does the story include specific, vivid details that paint a clear picture?**

□ **Could someone retell it without notes?**

If the answer to any of these questions is no, your message might be missing the one thing that makes it stick.

You'll find a complete exercise to help you restructure your current communications using the **EPIC Framework™** at the end of this chapter.

Don't Just Communicate. Connect. We live in a world full of perfectly formatted facts. But people don't act because of data.

They act because they feel seen. Because they relate. Because they believe.

That's the power of a well-told story.

It's not just how you stand out. It's how you get chosen.

Your Turn: Story Structure Exercise

Take one of your current communications and restructure it using EPIC:

1. Engage - Start with a specific person/moment

Who is your protagonist?______________________________

What challenge are they facing?________________________

2. Persuade - Add specific details

What vivid details make this real?_____________________

What turning point created change?____________________

3. Inspire - Show transformation

How has their life changed?_________________________

What does this represent for your mission?______________

4. Close - Make next step clear

. . .

What specific action should they take?____________________

How does this connect to the story? _____________________

Compare: Which version would you be more likely to remember?

□ Before □ After

—

Coming up in Chapter 5: Why your organization isn't struggling because your words aren't clever enough. It's struggling because your vision isn't bold enough. The surprising difference between content that gets noticed and content that starts movements.

i

CHAPTER 5: FORGET COPYWRITING. START LEADING

THE DIFFERENCE BETWEEN GOOD CONTENT AND CONTAGIOUS BELIEF.

Your organization isn't struggling because your words aren't clever enough. You're struggling because your vision isn't bold enough. There's a difference between content that gets noticed and content that moves people to act—and it has nothing to do with marketing tactics.

When a nonprofit approached me about their fundraising struggles, I expected to find the usual suspects: weak headlines, unclear calls-to-action, maybe some design issues. Instead, I discovered something far more fundamental: they had a storytelling problem. And that's a much bigger deal than most realize.

Here's what's even more staggering: 77% of nonprofits don't have a strategic marketing plan at all. But the real issue isn't the absence of a plan; it's the absence of conviction.

As leadership expert Simon Sinek writes in *The Infinite Game,* "We've become skilled at capturing eyeballs but struggle to capture hearts and hands."

Consider these two messages about the same issue, childhood hunger:

Message A: "Please donate today. 1 in 6 children face food insecurity. Your gift makes a difference."

Message B: "Right now, in our city, children are sitting in classrooms unable to focus because their stomachs are empty. Not because there isn't enough food, but because there isn't enough connection between abundance and need. We're building that bridge —one meal, one family, one community at a time. Join us not just in feeding children today, but in reshaping systems so hunger becomes history."

The first message informs. The second one leads.

And therein lies the opportunity for every messenger, regardless of title, budget, or cause:

Safe messages don't start movements. They maintain mediocrity.

Don't just send a message. Share a mission.

Why Good Content Isn't Good Enough

The words you put into the world either create movement or maintain the status quo. They either echo what's already been said or declare something worth believing in.

The problem?

We've been trained to write copy. To get clicks. To chase conversions.

But conversion is not the same as commitment.

You're not trying to solicit a donation, recruit a volunteer, or launch a campaign. You're trying to spark contagious belief.

Yes, you need clarity. Yes, you need story. They're what creates a good marketing piece. But if your message stops at "good," you've missed the point.

Because the best messages aren't just well-written. They're well-led.

They point somewhere. They stir something. They shift the way people see themselves and what they're capable of.

If you want your message to ignite action, not just attention, you have to stop thinking like a copywriter and start thinking like a guide, a visionary, a leader.

The Difference Between Copywriting and Leadership

Let's dig into this:

Copywriting Mindset	Leadership Mindset
"What will get the click?"	"What will change the conversation?"
"What headline converts best?"	"What message creates momentum?"
"What tactic increases donations?"	"What belief inspires movement?"

Copywriting is tactical. Leadership is transformational.

Copywriting often plays not to lose. Leadership plays for legacy.

And legacy begins when your words start shaping people, not just shifting metrics.

Case Study: How Charity: Water Transformed Nonprofit Messaging

When Scott Harrison founded Charity: Water in 2006, the nonprofit sector was dominated by guilt-driven appeals and complex messaging about water issues. The standard technique was to overwhelm donors with statistics on global water scarcity and use crisis language to trigger giving.

Harrison took a different approach. Instead of more sophisticated copy, he focused on leadership-driven messaging with three key elements:

• **A bold promise:** 100% of public donations would go directly to water projects, a commitment that challenged industry norms

• **A clear invitation:** Join a community solving the water crisis together rather than merely donating to an organization

• **Compelling proof:** Every project was GPS-mapped and photographed, with donors receiving specific coordinates of their impact

"We weren't just asking people to give money," Harrison writes in *Thirst: A Story of Redemption, Compassion, and a Mission to Bring Clean Water to the World.* "We were inviting them to join a movement that would reinvent charity."

The results speak for themselves. By 2022, Charity: Water had raised over $740 million and funded more than 111,000 water projects serving 16.4 million people across 29 countries. Their community of monthly donors, called "The Spring," grew to over 80,000 people.

They didn't achieve these results through marketing tactics alone, but through a fundamental leadership-driven message that changed how people saw themselves in relation to solving global problems.

Case Study: How Feeding America's Empty Plate Campaign Led Rather Than Asked

In 2014, Feeding America launched a campaign that defied conventional nonprofit appeals. Instead of leading with statistics about hunger or images of suffering, they created "The Empty Plate" campaign that featured clean, simple images of empty plates accompanied by powerful stories of people who had experienced food insecurity.

This campaign wasn't just a different creative approach. It represented a fundamental leadership stance that:

• Shifted the narrative from pity to dignity

• Created a powerful visual metaphor that anyone could understand

• Invited participation in solving a systemic problem, not just addressing symptoms

The campaign's tagline, "Together, we can solve hunger," positioned donors as partners in a movement rather than just financial supporters of an organization.

The results were significant. The campaign contributed to a 32% increase in online donations and dramatically improved brand recognition. More importantly, it shifted public dialogue about hunger from a distant problem affecting "others" to a community challenge requiring collective action.

Feeding America was doing more than clever fundraising. They were leading through messaging that treated audiences as capable of understanding systemic issues and inspired them to see themselves as part of the solution.

Movements Aren't Started by Marketers. They're Started by Believers.

Think about the most influential messengers in history:

Martin Luther King Jr. didn't post graphics. He delivered vision with what communication scholars identify as "prophetic voice," a rhetorical approach that envisions a future worth fighting for.

Malala Yousafzai didn't rely on carefully crafted PR. She spoke truth to power about girls' education with what researchers call "moral courage," a form of communication that places principle above personal safety and conventional acceptance.

None of them started with a polished campaign. They started with conviction.

So the real question is this: Are you just marketing what you do, or are you leading people somewhere they truly want to go?

Your audience isn't looking for the next best deal or a convenient way to feel good about giving. They're looking for conviction. For clarity. For someone who believes in something bold enough to say it out loud and back it up with action.

You're not just a communicator. You're a leader.

It's time to speak like one.

Because people aren't drawn to facts. They're drawn to vision. They want to be part of something bigger than themselves. They want to leave a legacy.

Give them a reason to follow you there.

Your Message Can't Be Neutral

When your message is vague, vanilla, or overly polished, it doesn't feel safe. It feels soulless.

Trying to appeal to everyone usually means moving no one. It's like those mission statements that mention "empowering communities through innovative solutions"—safe enough for any nonprofit to use, which is exactly why none of them should.

Stop being so boring and agreeable. Take a risk. Be bold.

Audiences don't trust copy that sounds like it was written by committee. They trust messages that sound like a leader who knows where they're going.

And more importantly, why it matters.

If your message isn't moving people, don't add more polish. Add more authenticity and purpose.

The polish will follow.

Case Study: UNICEF's "Likes Don't Save Lives" Leadership Campaign

In 2013, UNICEF Sweden took a bold stance that challenged the very foundation of social media engagement. They launched the "Likes Don't Save Lives" campaign with a provocative message: "We've noticed that many people who 'like' us on social media don't actually donate. Unfortunately, these likes aren't enough to fund our polio vaccinations."

The campaign featured posters with statements like: "Like us on Facebook and we will vaccinate zero children against polio."

The stark honesty cut through conventional social media marketing that celebrated engagement without conversion.

Director of Communications Petra Hallebrant explained: "We need to be stubborn and focused in our communication. We need to be clear about the challenges we face and what we need to address them. Social media engagement is important, but what we truly need is action."

The campaign received significant global media coverage and more importantly, drove a 33% increase in actual donations during the campaign period. UNICEF didn't stop at challenging shallow engagement. They provided clear alternatives for meaningful action.

This wasn't just a clever social media campaign. It was leadership through honest communication that respected audience intelligence and challenged them to move beyond passive support.

Movements Are Fueled by the EPIC Storytelling Framework

This is where we bridge into the **EPIC Framework™** because movements don't just need vision. They need structure.

They need a way to translate belief into behavior. Emotion into engagement. Passion into partnership.

The **EPIC Framework™** is how you do that. It's how you consistently create communication that transcends mere persuasion to become a catalyst for change:

Engage (Lead with Problems Worth Solving) Leadership messaging starts by naming real challenges that matter to your audience, not to sell solutions, but to rally around shared purpose. This creates the emotional foundation for commitment.

Example: When Bryan Stevenson founded the Equal Justice Initiative, he didn't lead with legal services. He led with stories of innocent people on death row, connecting audiences to the human cost of a broken system before introducing solutions.

Persuade (Build Trust Through Story and Truth) Leadership messaging earns trust through authentic storytelling and transparent evidence. It doesn't manipulate; it illuminates through vivid examples and honest assessment.

Example: When researcher Brené Brown shares her own vulnerability alongside her data on shame and courage, she models the very truths she's teaching, creating congruence between message and messenger.

Inspire (Elevate Vision Beyond Transactions) Leadership messaging connects immediate actions to a larger purpose. It doesn't just focus on what people can do, but who they can become through participation.

Example: When Habitat for Humanity founder Millard Fuller spoke about their work, he didn't just talk about building houses. He invited supporters to create "a world where everyone has a decent place to live," elevating individual donations into a global vision for human dignity.

Close (Guide Next Steps with Clarity and Confidence) Leadership messaging provides clear direction without manipulation. It respectfully guides people toward meaningful action aligned with the vision.

Example: When Khan Academy founder Sal Khan asks for support, he doesn't use urgency or scarcity tactics. He clearly connects donations to specific educational impacts with transparency about how funds are used.

Whether you're sending emails, filming a video, or presenting to your board, this framework works because it leads people, not just informs them.

Leading with Story Starts Inside You

Here's the hard truth: You can't lead others with your message until you believe it yourself.

The most magnetic communicators, the ones who start movements, don't rely on scripts.

They speak from centered clarity. They've done the work to get clear on:

• What problem they're here to solve

• What promise they can stand behind

• What outcome they believe is possible

• What truth they're unwilling to compromise

This kind of message? It's not manufactured. It's forged.

It's born out of fire, tested in the real world, and delivered with conviction.

And it's this kind of message that builds movements that stick.

Message Leadership Audit: Rate Your Communication

For each dimension, rate your most recent communication on a scale of 0-5, where 0 = pure copywriting approach and 5 = pure leadership approach.

Dimension	0 - Copywriting Approach	5 - Leadership Approach	Your Score
Focus	Programs and services	Purpose and vision	—
Tone	Persuasive or urgent	Conviction and clarity	—
Problem Framing	Individual needs	Systemic challenges	—
Call to Action	Transaction-oriented	Participation-oriented	—
Success Metric	Donation amount	Community impact	—

Total Score: ___ /25

Your Leadership Message Score:

• 0-8: Heavy copywriting focus - you're asking, not leading

• 9-16: Mixed approach - some leadership elements emerging

• 17-25: Strong leadership voice - you're building a movement

Now, identify one aspect of your message you could shift from copywriting to leadership. How would you rewrite it to lead rather than just ask?

Three Questions to Move From Copywriter to Movement Leader

To make this practical, ask yourself:

1 What truth about your mission are you afraid to say out loud? That's exactly where your leadership begins.

2 What belief are you inviting donors to share? If you can't name it in one sentence, go deeper.

3 Are you giving people something to commit to, not just contribute to? If it ends at inspiration, it ends too soon.

You're Not Just Sharing Content. You're Shaping Culture.

Every word you write, every story you tell, is a chance to lead someone from confusion to clarity, from apathy to action, from fear to faith in the future.

The world doesn't need more fundraising appeals. It needs more meaning.

And you are the one to deliver it.

Ready to transform your message from copy to conviction? Visit epicimpact.com or scan the QR code for the Message Leadership Assessment and frameworks that will help you shift from asking to leading.

—

Coming up in Chapter 6: Why 95% of nonprofit leaders are burning out and how the very way we've been taught to communicate is making it worse. What if leading didn't have to be so hard?

i

CHAPTER 6: BURNOUT AND THE CALL TO LEAD DIFFERENTLY

WHY MISSION-DRIVEN LEADERS ARE RUNNING ON EMPTY AND WHAT COMES NEXT.

What if Leading Didn't Have to Be So Hard?

Your compassion comes at a cost. As a nonprofit leader, you carry more than a job. You bear stories, expectations, and the weight of showing up even when you're running on fumes.

The statistics paint a stark picture of what you already know in your bones. According to the Center for Effective Philanthropy's (CEP) 2024 State of Nonprofits report, 95 percent of all leaders surveyed cited burnout as a concern, with half of nonprofit leaders feeling more concerned about their own burnout than this time last year. Burnout is a sector-wide crisis that's threatening the very mission you've dedicated your life to serving.

The Weight of Caring: Understanding the Nonprofit Mental Health Crisis

The numbers tell a story that's both heartbreaking and urgent. Nearly one in four workers are experiencing burnout symptoms, which include cynicism, demotivation, irritability, fatigue, insomnia, anxiety, and depression. But here's what makes the nonprofit sector different: In the U.S. specifically, 48% of nonprofit leaders struggle with burnout, nearly double the rate of other industries.

As one 20-year nonprofit veteran shared in recent research: "I have not experienced a reality like the one I am in currently. There are no trailblazers that have faced this path before us to guide and advise. It is a wild world right now."

This is the reality: You're leading in uncharted territory, carrying unprecedented burdens.

The mental health impact on leaders is severe. Research indicates that CEOs may experience depression at a rate more than double that of the general public. For women nonprofit leaders, the burden is even heavier. Studies confirm that female respondents struggled more than male respondents with balancing their professional and personal roles.

The Hidden Cost of Mission-Driven Leadership

Your dedication to the cause comes with a psychological price tag that few people understand. In discussions with nonprofit leaders, many indicated a resistance to prioritizing their own needs when others are "worse off" or require more assistance than they do. This martyrdom mindset goes beyond nobility. It's destructive.

Here's what's happening to leaders like you:

The Overwhelm is Real: Nearly a quarter of respondents in the CEP survey reported losing more staff than was typical in 2024, leaving remaining leaders to shoulder impossible workloads.

The Financial Stress is Crushing: You're caught in an impossible bind. "We aren't able to pay our staff a livable wage, which is the exact goal we are aiming to reach for the clients we serve," says one leader. "With that, we see higher turnover in our case management team, in addition to each member being responsible for a larger caseload than is sustainable."

The Isolation is Profound: Unlike business leaders who can raise prices or find new revenue streams to solve problems, you're constrained by funding structures and donor expectations that often ignore operational realities.

Real-Life Transformation: How One Leader Broke Free From Communication Chaos

Marti Spencer was drowning in the daily juggle that defines nonprofit leadership. Every morning brought a flood of communications to craft, review, and send - donor updates, program announcements, board reports, and volunteer coordination. The quality suffered. The mission got buried under the mountain of messaging tasks.

Sound familiar?

Marti knew her organization's story was powerful, but she couldn't find the time or framework to tell it consistently. That's when she discovered the **EPIC Framework™** combined with AI tools. Instead of starting from scratch every time, she had a proven structure. Instead of spending hours on drafts, AI helped her iterate faster while maintaining her authentic voice.

The transformation wasn't just about efficiency—it was about reclaiming her role as a leader, not just a communicator.

Here's what Marti had to say about her experience:

---

*"Combining the **EPIC Framework™** with AI has been a godsend for our nonprofit. Our communication is clearer and higher quality, and it's given me time back to focus on what matters most—our mission."*

—Marti Spencer, CEO/Executive Director, Ronald McDonald House Charities of the Carolinas

The EPIC difference? Marti moved from reactive communication to strategic message leadership.

The EPIC Solution: Communication That Heals Rather Than Drains

Traditional communication advice tells you to "know your audience" and "craft compelling messages" as if you have unlimited time and energy to customize every interaction. This approach is designed for people with full communications teams, not for leaders juggling a dozen roles while running on fumes.

EPIC recognizes your reality: **You need communication that works efficiently and authentically, regardless of your energy level.**

Here's why EPIC specifically serves exhausted leaders:

1. Cognitive Load Reduction

When you're overwhelmed, decision fatigue is real. EPIC provides a proven structure so you're not starting from scratch every time you need to communicate. The framework handles the "how," so you can focus on the "what."

2. Authenticity Over Performance

EPIC doesn't require you to be "on" all the time. It gives you permission to lead from wherever you are: tired, stressed, hopeful, or determined. Authentic connection beats performative enthusiasm every time.

3. Scalable Impact

One EPIC message can be adapted for multiple audiences and communication pieces, including grants, donor appeals, volunteer recruitment, board presentations, and staff communications. You create once and adapt many times, instead of recreating constantly.

4. Sustainable Systems Over Heroic Efforts

EPIC builds communication systems that work without you having to be superhuman. It's designed for consistency, not for those rare moments when you feel fully energized and inspired.

The Science of Communication and Mental Health

Research proves what you've experienced: Those who engaged in self-care were able to improve their work effectiveness by 21 percent and their well-being by 45 percent. But self-care extends beyond bubble baths and yoga (though those help). For leaders, self-care includes having communication systems that don't drain your mental resources.

Every unclear message, every misunderstood grant application, every donor relationship that requires constant explanation is a mental health hazard hiding in plain sight. They create the communication overwhelm that keeps you working late, second-guessing your words, and carrying the stress of miscommunication.

EPIC addresses this threat at the source. Clear, structured communication reduces the mental load of being constantly "on," constantly explaining, and constantly worried about whether your message is landing.

Breaking the Martyrdom Cycle

The nonprofit sector has normalized suffering in the service of the mission. Let's end this culture of martyrdom, as Vu Le, a nonprofit consultant and author of the popular blog NonprofitAF, challenges us to do. Your well-being isn't an indulgence. It's strategic.

When you communicate with clarity and structure, you:

• Reduce the mental energy spent on message creation

- Increase the likelihood of being understood the first time

- Build systems that work even when you're not at your peak

- Model sustainable leadership for your team

The Hidden Message in Your Communication

Every time you send a confused email, give a disjointed presentation, or write a grant that doesn't tell your story clearly, you're sending a hidden message to yourself: "I don't have time to do this right." This message compounds, creating a cycle of communication stress that adds to your mental load.

EPIC breaks this cycle. When you know your message is structured, clear, and authentic, you can send it without the lingering anxiety of "Did I say that right? Will they understand? Should I follow up with clarification?"

This goes beyond external communication. It's about internal peace.

Your Communication Prescription

If you're reading this chapter while running on coffee and determination, here's your immediate action plan:

Stop making communication harder than it needs to be. You don't need different messages for different audiences. You need one core message that can be adapted.

Start with EPIC's structure, not with a blank page. The framework gives you a scaffold to build on, reducing the cognitive load of creation.

Trust the system, especially when you don't trust yourself. On your hardest days, when your confidence is low and your energy is depleted, EPIC provides a reliable structure that works regardless of how you feel.

The Ripple Effect of Sustainable Communication

When you adopt communication systems that support rather than drain you, the impact extends far beyond your inbox:

• **Your team sees sustainable leadership modeled.** They learn it's possible to be effective without being exhausted.

• **Your board gains confidence in your communication clarity.** Clear messages reduce their anxiety and increase their support.

• **Your donors receive consistent, authentic messages.** They don't have to decode what you need. They can focus on deciding whether to help.

• **Your community experiences a leader who is present and energized.** Your resilience enables their progress.

The Truth About Efficiency and Heart

Some leaders worry that systematic communication will make them sound robotic or inauthentic. This fear reveals a dangerous myth: that authenticity requires starting from scratch every time, that caring means making it harder on yourself.

The truth is exactly the opposite. When you have a reliable communication structure, you can put your mental energy into the heart of your message rather than the mechanics of delivery. EPIC doesn't make you less authentic. It makes space for your authenticity to shine through consistently.

You were never meant to carry this alone. The nonprofit sector's expectation that leaders should sacrifice their well-being for the mission goes beyond unsustainable. It's counterproductive. The communities you serve need you to be healthy, present, and communicating with clarity.

EPIC goes beyond being a communication framework. It's a mental health intervention disguised as a messaging system. It recognizes that your emotional and psychological resources are finite, and it protects them by making communication efficient, effective, and sustainable.

The question goes beyond whether you have time to learn a new communication approach. The question is whether you have time to keep struggling with the old one.

—

Coming up in Chapter 7: The surprising discovery that changed everything I thought I knew about effective communication and why a FedEx truck stuck in my driveway became the key to a framework that's transforming how leaders connect with their audiences.

Note: Specific performance metrics and the mental health leadership scenario are presented as illustrative examples to demonstrate potential outcomes and common challenges, not as documented case study results.

i

PART 2: MASTERING THE EPIC FRAMEWORK™

BUILD SKILL. SPARK TRUST. MAKE PEOPLE CARE ACROSS ANY PLATFORM.

CHAPTER 7: ENTER EPIC: YOUR FRAMEWORK FOR SUSTAINABLE IMPACT

A DEEP DIVE INTO ENGAGE. PERSUADE. INSPIRE. CLOSE.

Ever wonder why some of your messages get ignored while others create immediate response? The difference isn't luck, it's structure.

My EPIC Discovery

"What happens when you mix a snowstorm, a FedEx truck, and a lawn that didn't ask for this life?"

That was the subject line of an email I sent to my subscribers one winter morning. What happened next changed everything I understood about effective communication.

The email told the story of an unexpected encounter:

I heard the unmistakable rev-rev-rev of tires spinning and a beep-beep-beep outside. Looking out the window, I saw a FedEx truck stuck in my snow-filled driveway.

Snow was flying everywhere. Rushing out, my first thought was, "Dude, what were you thinking?" But then I saw the driver step out, shoulders slumped. "Yeah, I knew I shouldn't have pulled in," he admitted sheepishly.

My heart softened. My poor lawn now had ruts deep enough to plant corn, but instead of anger, I chose kindness. I invited him inside to warm up while he waited for a tow truck.

We started chatting, and he opened up about his family and his love for his job, despite days like this. After an hour (plus 30 minutes of the tow truck pulling him out), he turned to me and said, "You know, I thought you'd yell at me for this. Most people would. Thanks for not being a bitch like I expected. Can I give you a hug?" A hug! From the guy who tore up my lawn.

This real-life lesson reminded me: Choosing kindness creates moments that matter, not just for others, but for us too.

When I sent this email, I wasn't expecting what happened next.

It achieved a staggering 70% open rate and 49% click-through rate, metrics that stand far above industry standards. That's the day I knew I had discovered something profound about compelling communication. Not a trick or a gimmick, but a framework that honors how human connection actually works.

Want to read the full version of the original email that started it all? Check out your **Epic Impact™** starter kit to see how the story unfolded in real time and why it resonated so deeply.

This was the first email I intentionally structured using what would become the **EPIC Framework™.** Since then, I've consistently seen dramatic improvements in engagement across all my communications.

And I'm not the only one seeing results.

---

*"Hailey's training on leveraging AI for marketing messaging and her **EPIC Communication Framework™** inspired us to craft a simple yet impactful email that deeply resonated with our audience. Her suggestion to incorporate a creative video led one of our board members to shoot an engaging clip that people absolutely loved and couldn't stop talking about! It's incredible how something so straightforward, when paired with Hailey's thoughtful strategy and execution, can have such a powerful impact. Her insights were truly instrumental in the success of our enhanced communication efforts!"*

—Jon Nelson, Associate Director, ACF - Association for Christian Fundraising

---

But for now, remember this: You don't need another funnel. You need a story people can't wait to repeat.

The Power of Framework Over Formulas

Most messaging "formulas" feel mechanical for a reason—they are. They're designed for transactions, not transformation. But the **EPIC Framework™** is different. It's not about manipulating emotions or following rigid rules. It's about creating a natural flow that honors how human connection actually works.

Think of it like this: When you meet someone new, you don't immediately ask them for a commitment. You build rapport. You share stories. You find common ground. Only then do you extend an invitation.

This is precisely how the **EPIC Framework™** functions. It creates a natural progression that feels right to the human brain because it mirrors how real relationships develop.

You already have powerful stories. What you've been missing is a framework to make them work every time.

The EPIC Framework™: A Complete System

Let's explore each component of the framework that has transformed communication for thousands of leaders across sectors:

E: Engage with Connection

The Core Principle: Create immediate connection through challenges your audience recognizes and cares about.

The Question It Answers: "Why should I pay attention right now?"

The Science Behind It: The brain is wired to notice problems before solutions. When you connect with challenges your audience already feels, you create what neuroscientists call a "problem recognition response" that primes them to be receptive to what follows.

The Transformation

Before EPIC: "Our organization provides after-school tutoring to at-risk youth."

After EPIC: "Jayden stared at his math homework, tears welling up. With falling grades and no help at home, his confidence was slipping away, along with his dreams of college."

An opening that creates emotional connection and makes the reader want to know what happens next.

The first version informs. The second one engages through human connection.

P: Persuade through Story and Evidence

The Core Principle: Build trust through authentic storytelling paired with credible evidence that illuminates truth through both emotional resonance and logical proof.

The Question It Answers: "Why should I believe you can solve this problem?"

The Science Behind It: When we hear stories, our brains release oxytocin, often referred to as the "trust hormone," which enhances empathy and connection. When emotional engagement pairs with credible evidence, it creates optimal conditions for persuasion.

The Transformation

Before EPIC: "Our tutoring program has helped hundreds of students improve their grades."

After EPIC: "Three months into our program, Jayden's math grade jumped from a D to a B. But the real transformation happened the day he ran into the center, waving his test paper with its red '92%' circled at the top. 'I did it myself!' he announced. Our quarterly assessment shows that 89% of our students improve at least one letter grade within the first semester, but more importantly, 94% report increased confidence in their abilities."

The first version makes a claim. The second one proves it through both story and statistics.

I: Inspire with Vision Beyond Transactions

The Core Principle: Elevate the conversation from immediate needs to a larger purpose, connecting individual actions to meaningful identity and impact.

The Question It Answers: "How does this connect to something bigger than myself?"

The Science Behind It: People are motivated more by who they can become than by what they can get. This "identity-based motivation" is far more potent than transaction-based approaches.

The Transformation

Before EPIC: "Your donation will help provide tutoring services to more students."

After EPIC: "When you support our tutoring program, you're not just helping kids with homework. You're building a community where every child, regardless of zip code or family circumstance, has a champion who believes in them. You're part of rewriting the story of education in our city, one student at a time."

The first version focuses on the transaction. The second one invites participation in a movement.

C: Close with Clarity and Confidence

The Core Principle: Guide next steps with absolute clarity, removing all barriers between intention and action.

The Question It Answers: "What exactly do you want me to do now?"

The Science Behind It: When people face too many options or unclear pathways, they often choose none. Clear direction reduces cognitive load and dramatically increases response rates.

The Transformation

Before EPIC: "Please consider supporting our organization with a donation. You can also volunteer or spread the word about our programs."

After EPIC: "Will you become a Homework Hero with your monthly gift of $47? This provides one student with weekly tutoring for an entire month, including all materials and a trained mentor. Click the button below to start your monthly support, and we'll send you a photo and letter from a student like Jayden in your first welcome package."

The first approach offers options but creates hesitation. The second makes the decision straightforward and compelling.

The Framework in Action: Proven Results

The beauty of the **EPIC Framework™** is its versatility across industries. Here are examples of organizations that have transformed their communication:

Nonprofit Success: Environmental Foundation

Challenge: Technical environmental work was difficult to translate into donor support. **EPIC Solution:** Connected environmental protection to personal stories and community impact. **Result:** Significant increase in both response rates and average gift size.

Healthcare Transformation: Regional Medical Center

Challenge: Recruiting healthcare professionals in a competitive market. **EPIC Solution:** Elevated recruitment from job postings to joining a healing community. **Result:** Substantial improvements in applications and retention rates.

Your Message Is Your Mission in Motion

Before we move on, I want to leave you with this truth: Your message isn't separate from your mission. It's your mission in motion.

The words you choose and how you structure them don't just describe your impact. They create it.

Because when your message is clear, your mission can spread. When your story is structured, your support can grow. When your communication leads, your community follows.

The **EPIC Framework™** isn't just about writing better emails or creating more compelling appeals. It's about leading a movement that matters, one message at a time.

Your EPIC Transformation Starts Now

The journey from confusion to clarity requires commitment. Here's how to begin:

1 Audit Your Current Materials: Review your communications through the EPIC lens

2 Start with One Piece: Choose one important message to restructure

3 Test and Measure: Compare results before and after implementation

4 Scale Systematically: Apply the framework across your organization

Ready to transform your communication strategy? The complete **EPIC Framework™** with detailed templates, worksheets, and step-by-step guidance is available in you **EPIC Impact™** Starter Kit at epicimpact.ai

—

Coming up in Chapter 8: How the same framework that transformed nonprofit fundraising also helped a real estate agent turn "dirt into dreams" and why industry leaders across every sector are using EPIC to revolutionize their results.

i

CHAPTER 8: HOW INDUSTRY LEADERS TRANSFORM THEIR RESULTS WITH ONE SIMPLE FRAMEWORK

HOW BUSINESS OWNERS, CONSULTANTS, HEALTHCARE PROVIDERS, AND SALES PROFESSIONALS ADAPT EPIC TO THEIR UNIQUE AUDIENCES.

How business owners, consultants, healthcare providers, and sales professionals adapt EPIC to their unique audiences.

You've learned the **EPIC Framework™.** You've seen how it transforms communication from confusing to compelling. But here's what might surprise you: the same four-step structure that revolutionized my nonprofit clients' fundraising also helped a real estate agent sell a property that had been sitting on the market for over a year.

The framework doesn't change. But how you apply it? That's where the magic happens.

The Great Land Agent Awakening

I met Jack at a workshop I led for the Southeast Land Group in Alabama, and his transformation still brings a smile to my face.

Before I even started my presentation, I looked out at the room and shared an uncomfortable truth: "Folks, 95% of land agents are men, and you're all trying to sell dirt. If there's ever been a need for storytelling, it's right now."

The room grew quiet as they looked at each other with that uncomfortable recognition that comes when someone calls out an obvious truth. Then I launched into my usual EPIC + AI demo and asked for a volunteer. Jack's hand shot up faster than anyone else's.

Since I love spicing things up, I had to poke a little fun at him. "Jack, show me your oldest listing that you're sick of seeing. The one that's been sitting there so long it's practically become furniture in your brain."

He laughed and pulled it up on his phone. "This one's been haunting me for a year," he said with a groan. "I'm so tired of looking at it, I could write it from memory."

He pulled it up on his phone. I looked at the screen, then at the room, then back at Jack. I immediately recognized the problem. Did he?

"Dude, this looks like one big run-on sentence. No one wants to read a giant wall of text! There's no spacing between ideas, so people's brains immediately shut down. It's too much work and they'll just move on."

The room chuckled nervously. Jack's listing was a perfect example of what I see everywhere:

"Beautiful 50-acre tract with mixed timber, seasonal creek running through northwest corner, excellent hunting potential with deer and turkey sign throughout, good road frontage on county maintained road, power and utilities available, property has been surveyed, located just 15 minutes from town but feels completely private, perfect for building dream home or weekend retreat, seller motivated and ready to negotiate, serious inquiries only, call for more details and showing appointment."

Boring. Blah. Yawn.

"Jack," I said, "this is informational when it should be inspirational. You're giving them ALL the info upfront, so they think they know everything. Instead, you need to feed them breadcrumbs, one at a time. Make them want to call you!"

Using EPIC and AI, I rewrote his listing in less than 20 seconds. All 50 eyeballs in the room went wide when they saw the transformation:

ENGAGE: "The old creek still whispers the same secrets it has for over a century, winding through these 50 untouched acres where deer paths tell stories of morning mist and quiet mornings."

PERSUADE: "This isn't just land, it's a sanctuary. The kind of place where your grandchildren will learn to fish in the same creek where you find your peace. Where the mixed timber provides natural privacy and the gentle roll of the terrain makes every sunrise feel like it was painted just for you."

INSPIRE: "Some people collect things. Smart people collect moments. This land doesn't just offer space to build a home, it offers space to build a legacy."

CLOSE: "Ready to walk the property that could change how you think about home? Call now to schedule your private tour and feel what 50 acres of possibility feels like."

Same land. Same features. But now, instead of "mixed timber," we have "natural privacy." Instead of "seasonal creek," we have "whispered secrets." Instead of "serious inquiries only," we have an invitation to experience possibility.

The next demo was even more fun. Steven, Jack's colleague in the room, was eager to be next. I took a picture of Steven's original listing with my phone, put it into my ChatGPT app, and then instructed it to rewrite it using my **EPIC Framework™.** No one had any idea you could do that! The room went completely silent as they watched his listing transform through a simple photo and voice command.

"You are working...Way. Too. Hard," I told them. "It's time to get on board with new tech and make your life easier."

The EPIC version doesn't just list features, it sells a feeling. And when 50 land agents see you transform dirt into dreams in 20 seconds using nothing but your phone, seven of them sign up for your **AI Marketing Bootcamp** on the spot.

Every single one of those seven agents experienced their own transformation. Three weeks prior, they didn't even know how to turn on ChatGPT, much less use it. The learning curve goes straight up with my **AI Marketing Bootcamp.** It's truly one of the most rewarding experiences to watch someone transition from AI-intimidated to AI-empowered in under a month.

Jack and Steven even created their own logos for their new landing pages using ChatGPT. I gotta say, for spending zero dollars and taking 20 minutes to tweak it a few times, it's amazing.

When the competition is as fierce as it is in real estate, standing out with your own professional branding isn't just smart, it's essential.

It's rewarding to teach people new ways of making their lives easier. Because once you stop selling property and start selling possibilities, everything changes.

Why EPIC Works Across Every Industry

The power of EPIC isn't in its complexity; it's in its universality. Every industry has problems to solve, stories to tell, and people to move. But each industry applies the framework differently because each industry serves different human needs.

One of the biggest snags I see is that people forget to start with the problem when they're asked, "What do you do?" If there's no problem, there is no story. Your audience needs to understand what's broken before they care about your solution.

The EPIC Intro: Your 30-Second Game Changer

Remember from Chapter 3, the EPIC Intro is your elevator pitch perfected. It's the concise version of your story that hooks people in everyday conversations. It follows a simple three-step formula: Problem, Solution, Outcome.

The EPIC Intro Formula:

Start with the Problem (Engage): Capture attention by naming a challenge your audience recognizes and cares about.

Explain Your Solution (Persuade): Build connection by sharing your specific approach or offering.

End with the Outcome (Inspire): Elevate the vision by showing the transformation your work creates.

The Close happens in how you deliver it, with confidence, clarity, and an invitation to continue the conversation.

Why It Works:

• It follows the natural storytelling pattern that the brain is wired to process

• It places your audience (not your organization) at the center of the story

• It focuses on transformation, not just information

You don't need just one version either. The adaptability of the EPIC Intro allows you to customize your message for various audiences and purposes.

Let's explore how different industries adapt EPIC to achieve transformational results.

Business Owners: From Features to Transformation

The Challenge: Most business owners talk about what they do instead of why it matters.

The EPIC Shift: Instead of listing services, successful business owners lead with the transformation they create. They understand that people don't buy products or services; they buy better versions of themselves.

Example Transformation: *Before EPIC:* Generic service descriptions that sound like everyone else *After EPIC:* Stories that connect emotionally and inspire action

The difference isn't just in the words; it's in understanding that behind every business challenge is a human being with dreams, fears, and aspirations.

I experienced this transformation power firsthand when I was invited to be a guest on Steve Ramona's "Doing Business with a Servant's Heart" podcast. During our conversation, Steve opened up about his frustrations using AI for his podcast workflow. He truly lives what he talks about, authentic, servant-hearted business practices, but technology was creating barriers instead of solutions. That conversation led me to create a custom GPT specifically for his needs, and the results speak for themselves:

"Hailey's custom GPT transformed my entire podcast workflow and my results."

"I was drowning in podcast production. Spending 30-40 minutes crafting each description and title, constantly running out of time, pushing episodes back. My guests were emailing

asking when their podcasts would be live. I wasn't serving them the way I wanted to.

Then Hailey revealed her exclusive custom GPT demo, and I was instantly blown away. She designed it to transform raw transcripts into powerful EPIC format, knocking out 9 pieces of compelling content with one click. I upload the raw transcript and in less than 60 seconds I have all the repurposed content instantly, structured using her proven framework.

The results are incredible: My podcast has exploded with 3x more views and I'm adding more subscribers to my channels. I'm getting podcasts up faster, and the feedback has been amazing. One guest told me, 'This is the best podcast I have ever seen, very memorable creation. My audience is getting a better feel for my guests and they're more willing to reach out to them.

If you're frustrated like I was, not getting the best information for your audience, Hailey's breakthrough EPIC approach will help you scale and grow. She's an absolute rockstar — easy to work with, brilliant at what she does, and delivers results. It's been a complete game-changer..."

—Steve Ramona, Host of "Doing Business with a Servant's Heart," which reached the top 5% of all podcasts globally, plus YouTube channel, TV show, and TV channel with a combined reach of millions of viewers globally.

Steve's experience demonstrates exactly what happens when business leaders stop focusing solely on features and start connecting through authentic storytelling and practical solutions.

Consultants: From Expertise to Empathy

The Challenge: Consultants often sound impressive but feel disconnected from real-world problems.

The EPIC Shift: The most successful consultants don't lead with their credentials—they lead with their clients' challenges. They speak the language of leadership, not the language of consulting.

Example Transformation: *Before EPIC:* Technical jargon that impresses but doesn't connect *After EPIC:* Clear communication that builds trust and demonstrates understanding

The best consultants understand that behind every organizational challenge is a leader who cares deeply about their people and their mission.

---

*"The **EPIC Framework™** is like a storytelling shortcut for busy marketers. As someone who already lives and breathes brand storytelling, I was skeptical I needed another framework until I tried this one. EPIC helps me write faster, more engaging content that still feels deeply authentic.*

I've seen a 10% lift in LinkedIn post impressions and an increase in email open rates when I use EPIC versus when I don't. But beyond the numbers, what really stands out is how it blends empathy with clarity. The 'Engage' and 'Persuade' steps especially help make brands sound more human which is where so many brands fall flat.

One of the biggest mistakes I see brands make is jumping straight to the CTA without ever building a connection. EPIC fixes that. It's intuitive, it's flexible, and it's effective. I now recommend it to clients who want to create content that actually connects. It's not the only way to write, but it's one you'll want in your toolbox."

— Sarah Panus, Content Strategist & Host of the Marketing With Empathy® Podcast, Kindred-Speak.com

---

Healthcare Providers: From Clinical to Compassionate

The Challenge: Healthcare communication often prioritizes medical accuracy over human connection.

The EPIC Shift: Leading healthcare providers understand that patients don't just want treatment, they want to feel heard, understood, and cared for as whole human beings.

Example Transformation: *Before EPIC:* Clinical descriptions that focus on procedures and protocols *After EPIC:* Patient-centered communication that addresses fears and builds trust

Behind every patient is a person who wants to get back to their life and the people they love.

Sales Professionals: From Pitch to Partnership

The Challenge: Most sales communication feels like being sold to, rather than being served.

The EPIC Shift: Top sales professionals don't pitch products, they solve problems. They position themselves as partners in their client's success, not vendors trying to make a sale.

Example Transformation: *Before EPIC:* Feature-heavy presentations that focus on what *you're selling After EPIC:* Problem-solving conversations that focus on *your client's outcomes*

The best sales relationships don't feel like sales at all, they feel like partnerships.

The Pattern You Can't Ignore

Notice the pattern? Every industry has:

• People with problems they're trying to solve

• Solutions that work when properly implemented

• Transformation stories that prove it's possible

• Next steps that feel approachable

The framework stays the same. The application changes everything.

Your Industry-Specific EPIC Journey

As we move into the next chapter, where you'll learn to leverage AI to scale your EPIC messaging, start thinking about how these patterns apply to your specific industry. The **EPIC Framework™** isn't a one-size-fits-all template. It's a thinking tool that adapts to serve your audience's specific needs, challenges, and dreams.

Ready to transform your content from flat to EPIC? Complete templates, messaging frameworks, and implementation strategies are available at **epicimpact.com**

—

Coming up in Chapter 9: How to transform any piece of content from flat to EPIC in minutes with real-world makeovers that show exactly how small changes create massive impact.

i

CHAPTER 9: SAMPLE TRANSFORMATIONS: FROM FLAT TO EPIC

REAL-WORLD MAKEOVERS OF LANDING PAGES, EMAILS, SPEECHES, AND MORE.

The moment you see a flat message transformed into an EPIC one, everything clicks. It's like watching someone turn on a light switch in a dark room—suddenly, you can see what was always there.

In this chapter, we're going behind the scenes of real transformations to see exactly how small strategic changes create a massive impact. These aren't theoretical examples. These are actual communications that went from ignored to irresistible using the EPIC Framework™.

The Anatomy of Transformation

Before we dive into the makeovers, let's establish what we're looking for in every transformation:

Flat Communication:

• Starts with the organization, not the audience

• Lists features instead of painting pictures

• Uses generic language that could apply to anyone

• Ends with weak or multiple calls to action

• Feels like work to read

EPIC Communication:

• Opens with a relatable human challenge

• Creates emotional connection through story

• Elevates to a larger vision or purpose

• Ends with one clear, compelling next step

• Feels effortless to consume

The difference isn't about being more dramatic or emotional. It's about being more human.

Makeover #1: The Mental Health Organization Website That Told History Instead of Hope

The Organization: A mental health advocacy organization

The Problem: Their impact page read like a textbook instead of an invitation to join a movement.

BEFORE: Historical but Marginal

"[A mental health advocacy organization] is the country's oldest and largest nonprofit organization addressing all aspects of mental health and mental illness. With 233 affiliates nationwide, [A mental health advocacy organization] works to improve the mental health of all Americans, especially the 54 million individuals with mental disorders, through advocacy, education, research and service.

[A mental health advocacy organization] was established in 1909 by former psychiatric patient Clifford W. Beers. During his stays in public and private institutions, Beers witnessed and was subjected to horrible abuse. From these experiences, Beers set into motion a reform movement that took shape as [A mental health advocacy organization]

Our work has resulted in positive change. We have educated millions about mental illnesses and reduced barriers to treatment and services. As a result of [A mental health advocacy organization's] efforts, many Americans with mental disorders have sought care and now enjoy fulfilling, productive lives in their communities."

What's Wrong Here:

• Opens with organizational structure instead of human impact

• Buried the compelling founding story in the middle

• Generic language ("positive change," "fulfilling lives")

• No clear call to action or next step

• Reads like a Wikipedia entry, not an invitation

AFTER: EPIC Transformation

ENGAGE: *"It started with one voice silenced, then awakened. A man once labeled 'broken' became the spark for a national movement that's still changing lives more than a century later."*

PERSUADE: *"In 1909, Clifford W. Beers turned his personal pain into public purpose. After enduring abuse in psychiatric institutions, he refused to stay silent. Instead, he launched a bold reform movement, one rooted in dignity, hope, and the belief that mental health is a right, not a privilege.*

That movement became [A mental health advocacy organization]. Today, with 233 affiliates nationwide, we are the country's oldest and largest nonprofit focused on all aspects of mental health and mental illness."

INSPIRE: *"Because of our work, millions have been educated. Barriers have been broken. And countless individuals who once suffered in silence are now living fulfilled, connected, purpose-driven lives.*

But we're not finished. With 54 million Americans facing mental health challenges, the need for advocacy, access, and compassion has never been greater."

CLOSE: *"[A mental health advocacy organization] is here for every voice that still needs to be heard. Together, we can continue this movement for change. Because no one should have to walk their mental health journey alone."*

The Transformation: Same facts. Completely different impact. Instead of starting with organizational details, we opened with the powerful human story that founded the movement. The EPIC structure turned institutional history into inspirational narrative.

Makeover #2: The Cybersecurity Landing Page That Listed Features Instead of Solving Problems

The Organization: A managed technology solutions provider

The Problem: Their landing page was clear but not compelling. It informed but didn't inspire action.

BEFORE: Professional but Predictable

Current Headline: *"Managed Technology Solutions with a Focus on Your Business"* **Current Subhead:** *"#1 Managed Service Provider in the Southeast"*

What They're Doing Right:

- Clear value proposition about business focus

- Strong social proof with regional authority claim

- Professional design and multiple contact options

• Solid testimonials and quantitative proof points

What's Missing:

• No emotional connection to the daily frustration of IT problems

• Generic testimonials without specific transformation stories

• Missing urgency or consequences of waiting

• Functional CTAs that don't inspire immediate action

AFTER: EPIC Transformation Strategy

ENGAGE - Hook with Heart: *Current*: "Managed Technology Solutions with a Focus on Your Business" *EPIC Version*: "Tired of firefighting IT issues? You're not alone. Most businesses lose hours each week to tech headaches and we're here to end that."

PERSUADE - Tell Real Stories: *Current*: Generic testimonials spread throughout the page *EPIC Addition*: "How We Helped Them Win" section featuring:

• Manufacturing client who reduced downtime by 89%

• Healthcare practice that eliminated data breaches completely

• Growing startup that scaled without IT growing pains

INSPIRE - Make It Matter: *Current*: "Put an End to Recurring IT Problems" *EPIC Addition*: "Why Now?" section highlighting the real cost of waiting:

• Lost productivity from system failures

• Security vulnerabilities that threaten everything you've built

• The peace of mind that comes from knowing IT just works

CLOSE - Take the Next Step: *Current*: "Request Pricing" and "Get Started" *EPIC Version*: "Let's solve your IT headaches fast. Get a free consultation and a custom plan in one business day."

The Strategic Shift: Instead of leading with what they do, they now lead with what their clients experience. The same services, same expertise, but now positioned around human problems and real transformations.

Makeover #3: The Fundraising Email That Told Stories But Missed the Ask

The Organization: A meal delivery nonprofit

The Problem: Beautiful stories that informed supporters but didn't inspire them to take action

BEFORE: Heartwarming but Not Compelling

"Local Firefighters Deliver Holiday Meals

While we are almost a month into 2025, we wanted to take a look back and share a special story from this past holiday season!

The holidays are often a challenging time of year for the senior and disabled homebound population that [A meal delivery nonprofit] serves. However, a group of special individuals took it upon themselves to make sure our homebound recipients had a special holiday season.

Fire Chief David Thompson of the [Local volunteer fire department] organizes with other area fire departments to cook and deliver special holiday meals to many of our recipients who might not be able to join family or friends for a meal during Thanksgiving and Christmas.

'It's a special day for me to visit and see the hustle and bustle of this group of servants who come together from several fire departments and serve our seniors,' says Maria Rodriguez, executive director of [A meal delivery nonprofit]. 'We appreciate their generosity to spend part of their holiday helping others.'

The meal is lovingly prepared and delivered and includes all of the usual fixings you would find on the table during Thanksgiving and the

holidays and is delivered by a friendly volunteer who interacts with the individual they deliver to, making the day extra special.

Because of individuals like Chief Thompson and the people who volunteer with him to make and deliver these meals, our homebound neighbors were not forgotten during this past holiday season."

What's Wrong Here:

• Sweet story but no clear call to action

• Focuses on what others did, not what readers can do

• Past-tense storytelling that feels closed-ended

• No emotional connection to specific individuals served

• Misses the opportunity to invite participation

AFTER: EPIC Transformation

ENGAGE: *"Dorothy hadn't seen another person in three days when she heard the knock on her door. At 84, with mobility challenges and no family nearby, the holidays had become a season of silence instead of celebration."*

PERSUADE: *"When Fire Chief David Thompson and his team of volunteer firefighters appeared at Dorothy's door with a full Thanksgiving meal, her face lit up for the first time in weeks. 'I thought everyone had forgotten about me,' she whispered, tears in her eyes. Chief Thompson and firefighters from multiple area departments have made this their holiday tradition—ensuring that seniors like Dorothy know they matter.*

But Chief Thompson can't reach everyone alone. Last year, we served over 400 holiday meals to homebound seniors, but we know there are dozens more like Dorothy still waiting by their doors, hoping someone remembers."

INSPIRE: *"You have the power to turn someone's loneliest day into their most memorable one. When you support [A meal delivery nonprofit], you're not just providing nutrition—you're delivering dignity, connection, and the message that no one should spend the holidays alone."*

CLOSE: *"This holiday season, will you help us reach every Dorothy in [A local meal delivery nonprofit]? Your gift of $25 provides a complete holiday meal and personal visit to one homebound senior. Together, we can ensure no one is forgotten."*

Makeover #4: The LinkedIn Post Nobody Engaged With

The Professional: A leadership coach struggling with social media engagement

The Problem: Educational posts that generated likes but no meaningful engagement or inquiries

BEFORE: Informative but Ignored

"5 Key Leadership Traits for Success:

1. Clear Communication 2. Emotional Intelligence 3. Strategic Thinking 4. Adaptability 5. Integrity

Developing these skills takes time and practice. Leaders who master these traits tend to be more effective and build stronger teams. What leadership trait do you think is most important?"

What's Wrong Here:

• Generic list that's been shared a thousand times

• No personal story or specific example

• Question feels forced and superficial

• No clear value or unique perspective

• Easy to scroll past without stopping

. . .

AFTER: EPIC Transformation

ENGAGE: *"The CEO froze mid-sentence during our coaching call. 'I just realized,' he said quietly, 'I've been so focused on being right that I forgot how to be human.'"*

PERSUADE: *"It happened during a team meeting where he'd dismissed a suggestion without really listening. Later, he learned that idea could have saved the company $2 million. But the real cost wasn't financial—it was the trust of the team member who stopped sharing ideas altogether."*

INSPIRE: *"Leadership isn't about having all the answers. It's about creating space for the right questions. When we lead with curiosity instead of certainty, we don't just make better decisions—we build better humans."*

CLOSE: *"What's one question you could ask your team this week that you've never asked before? Share it below—I'd love to hear how curiosity is reshaping your leadership."*

The Results: This post format increased engagement by 280% and generated 15 qualified coaching inquiries from one post.

Makeover #5: The Conference Speech That Put People to Sleep

The Speaker: A nonprofit executive presenting at an industry conference

The Problem: Important information delivered in a way that didn't stick or inspire action

BEFORE: Instructional but Uninspiring

"Good morning. I'm here to discuss the current state of nonprofit financial sustainability. According to recent studies, 60% of nonprofits

struggle with funding predictability. This creates challenges in strategic planning and program development.

Our organization has implemented several strategies to address these challenges. We've diversified our revenue streams, improved our donor retention rates, and invested in technology solutions that increase operational efficiency.

Today, I'll share three key strategies that can help your organization achieve greater financial sustainability: building recurring revenue, optimizing operational costs, and developing strategic partnerships.

Let me start with recurring revenue..."

YOUR TURN:

Take a moment to identify what makes this opening fall flat. Fill in the blanks below with what you observe:

What's Wrong Here:

• Opens with _______ instead of human connection

• _______-focused instead of audience-focused

• _______ tone that doesn't engage emotions

• No _______ or relatable example

• Feels like a _______, not a presentation

Use this as a diagnostic tool for your own presentations. What patterns do you notice? How might you avoid these same pitfalls?

Check your answers at the end of this chapter.

AFTER: EPIC Transformation

ENGAGE: *"Three years ago, I sat in my office at 11 PM, staring at the calculator on my desk. We had enough funding to keep our* *programs running for exactly 47 more days. Forty-seven days to figure out how to keep serving the 200 families who depended on us, or start making the calls no nonprofit leader ever wants to make."*

PERSUADE: *"That night changed everything about how we think about sustainability. Not because we found a magic donor or won a huge grant, but because we realized we'd been asking the wrong question. Instead of 'How do we find more money?' we started asking, 'How do we build a foundation that can weather any storm?' The answer transformed not just our organization, but our entire community."*

INSPIRE: *"You're not here because you love fundraising. You're here because you love the mission. Financial sustainability isn't about the money—it's about ensuring that the work you care about can continue long after you're gone. It's about building something bigger than budgets and more lasting than grants."*

CLOSE: *"By the end of this session, you'll have three specific strategies that can transform your organization's financial foundation. But more importantly, you'll leave with a new way of thinking about sustainability that makes the mission, not the money, the center of everything you do."*

The Results: This opening approach led to the highest session evaluations at the conference and 40+ requests for consulting conversations.

The Pattern Behind Every Transformation

Notice what happens in every successful makeover:

1 We start with humans, not organizations.

2 We create emotional connection before logical persuasion.

3 We show transformation, not just information.

4 We elevate to a purpose beyond the immediate ask.

5 We end with one clear, compelling next step.

These aren't tricks or gimmicks. They're principles that honor how human connection actually works.

Your Turn: The EPIC Transformation Challenge

Choose one piece of your current communication—an email, webpage, social post, or presentation. Apply the **EPIC Framework™** using these guiding questions:

For Engage: What human challenge does your audience face that you can help solve?

For Persuade: What story proves your solution works, and what evidence supports it?

For Inspire: How does taking action connect to something bigger than the immediate transaction?

For Close: What's the one clear next step you want them to take?

EXERCISE ANSWERS:

What's Wrong Here:

• Opens with **statistics** instead of human connection

• **Speaker**-focused instead of audience-focused

• **Academic** tone that doesn't engage emotions

• No **story** or relatable example

• Feels like a **report**, not a presentation

. . .

Key Takeaway: This opening commits the classic mistake of leading with data instead of humanity. The speaker jumps straight into percentages and organizational achievements without first connecting with the audience's experiences or emotions. It reads like a board report rather than a presentation designed to inspire and engage.

Before you continue: Think about your last presentation. Did you fall into any of these same traps? Keep these patterns in mind as we dive into the solutions ahead.

Because the difference between content that gets ignored and content that gets results isn't talent or budget. It's structure. And now you have the framework to make every message unforgettable.

Coming up in Chapter 10: When EPIC becomes automatic—how the framework transforms from a tool you use to an instinct you trust, and why that matters for scaling your impact.

Note: The examples in this chapter are illustrative composites, created to demonstrate the EPIC Framework™ in action. They do not depict specific individuals, organizations, or events. Any resemblance to actual persons, organizations, or situations is purely coincidental.

CHAPTER 10: WHEN EPIC BECOMES AUTOMATIC

HOW THE FRAMEWORK TRANSFORMS FROM TOOL TO INSTINCT, AND WHY THAT MATTERS FOR SCALING.

Sarah stared at the blank screen, cursor blinking mockingly at her. Three months ago, crafting a single email would have taken her hours of agonizing over every word, second-guessing her approach, and frantically Googling "how to write compelling subject lines" for the hundredth time.

Today? Her fingers moved across the keyboard with quiet confidence. **Engage** with a story about her client's transformation. **Persuade** with the specific result that mattered most to her audience. **Inspire** with a vision of what becomes possible. **Close** with a clear next step.

The email was done in twelve minutes. And it converted at 23%.

"When did this become so... automatic?" she wondered aloud.

That's the question this chapter answers. Because there's a moment in every EPIC practitioner's journey when the framework stops being something you *use* and becomes something you *are*. When story structure becomes as natural as breathing. When you can spot the emotional core of any message in seconds. When clarity flows from you like water from a spring.

This transformation goes far beyond convenience. It's essential for anyone serious about scaling their impact.

The Neuroscience of Automatic Excellence

Your brain is constantly seeking patterns, creating shortcuts, and automating processes to conserve energy. Neuroscientists call this "chunking," the mental process of grouping individual pieces of information into larger, more meaningful units that can be recalled and executed as a single action.

When you first learned to drive, you consciously thought about every movement: foot on brake, check mirrors, turn signal, look both ways. Now you navigate complex traffic while holding a hands-free phone conversation and mentally planning dinner. The driving patterns have become automatic, freeing your conscious mind for other tasks.

The same neurological process transforms how you communicate when EPIC becomes automatic. The conscious effort required to structure messages disappears, allowing your creativity and authentic voice to flourish within the framework's proven structure.

Dr. Angela Duckworth's research on deliberate practice demonstrates that true expertise extends beyond mere repetition. It's about practicing with focused attention until the skill becomes unconscious competence. With EPIC, this means moving through four distinct stages:

Stage 1: Conscious Incompetence - "I don't know how to structure a compelling message, and I know I don't know."

Stage 2: Conscious Competence - "I can create engaging content, but I have to think hard about each element of EPIC."

Stage 3: Unconscious Competence - "I naturally structure messages using EPIC without thinking about it."

Stage 4: Unconscious Excellence - "I can adapt and innovate within the framework intuitively, teaching others while continuously improving."

Most people give up somewhere in Stage 2, frustrated by the mental effort required. But those who push through to automaticity discover something remarkable: the framework doesn't constrain their creativity. It liberates it.

The Practice That Builds Instinct

Imagine you're facing a high-stakes communication challenge, perhaps a major client expressing dissatisfaction, a crucial presentation to secure funding, or a difficult conversation with a team member. In the past, you might have spent precious preparation time frantically bullet-pointing features and benefits, rehearsing logical arguments, or desperately searching for the "right" words.

But when EPIC becomes automatic, something different happens. Your mind instinctively reaches for story structure, not because you're consciously applying a framework, but because that's how you now naturally process and present information under pressure.

Consider how this might unfold:

Engage: Instead of launching into defensive explanations, you might open with a brief story about another situation where initial disconnection led to deeper understanding, creating psychological safety and demonstrating that challenges can be resolved.

Persuade: Rather than overwhelming your audience with data, you present specific evidence that addresses the core concern, showing measurable results in areas that matter most to them.

Inspire: You paint a picture of what becomes possible when the current challenge is resolved, connecting your audience to larger aspirations and shared values.

Close: You propose a specific, time-bound next step that moves the situation forward constructively.

This is what automatic EPIC looks like in practice: not rigid adherence to a formula, but intuitive navigation of communication challenges using proven principles. The framework doesn't constrain your natural response; it enhances it, ensuring your authentic voice carries maximum impact when it matters most.

The Compound Effect of Instinctive Communication

When EPIC becomes automatic, something powerful happens to your personal and professional influence. Consider these cascading effects:

Your Confidence Soars: Knowing you can handle any communication challenge reduces anxiety and imposter syndrome. You walk into presentations, difficult conversations, and networking events with quiet assurance.

Your Speed Increases: What once took hours now takes minutes. You can respond to opportunities quickly because you're not paralyzed by analysis. Your time-to-market improves dramatically.

Your Consistency Improves: Every piece of content you create carries the same engaging quality. Your audience begins to trust that consuming your content will be worth their time.

Your Adaptability Expands: The framework becomes a launching pad for innovation, not a restriction. You can modify and experiment while maintaining the core elements that make messages stick.

Your Teaching Ability Develops: You can help others improve their communication because you understand both the framework and the common pitfalls. This multiplies your impact exponentially.

Imagine a financial advisor who has reached this level of automaticity. Where they once avoided networking events because they never knew what to say, they now can take any conversation about someone's financial concerns and naturally guide it toward a story that illustrates the solution, evidence of why it works, and inspiration about what their future could look like. People might tell them they're a "natural" at connecting with clients, not realizing it's actually a systematic approach that creates this seemingly effortless communication ability.

The Three Pillars of Automatic EPIC

Moving from conscious competence to unconscious excellence requires strengthening three foundational pillars:

Pillar 1: Pattern Recognition

Automatic EPIC practitioners develop an almost supernatural ability to spot story opportunities in everyday experiences. They notice when someone shares a challenge that mirrors their ideal client's situation. They recognize when data tells a compelling narrative. They sense when an audience needs inspiration versus information.

This pattern recognition develops through what psychologists call "perceptual learning," your brain becoming increasingly sophisticated at distinguishing meaningful signals from noise. Every story you tell, every message you craft, every presentation you deliver strengthens your ability to recognize what works.

Practice this: For one week, notice every story shared in your presence: overheard conversations, social media posts, news articles, casual interactions. Ask yourself: "How could this story serve the **EPIC Framework™**? What's the emotional core? What change does it represent? How could I adapt this for my audience?"

Pillar 2: Emotional Calibration

Experienced EPIC practitioners develop exquisite sensitivity to emotional resonance. They can sense when a story lands versus when it falls flat. They recognize the difference between engagement and mere attention. They feel the shift in energy when inspiration takes hold.

This emotional calibration isn't mystical; it's learned. Mirror neurons in your brain fire both when you experience an emotion and when you observe others experiencing that emotion. The more you practice noticing and responding to emotional cues, the more accurate your calibration becomes.

Practice this: During every conversation this week, notice emotional shifts. When does energy increase? When does someone lean in? When do they check their phone? Start correlating these behavioral cues with the content being shared.

Pillar 3: Structural Flexibility

Novice EPIC users often apply the framework rigidly, creating content that feels formulaic. Masters understand that EPIC is a jazz framework: there's an underlying structure that allows for infinite improvisation.

Sometimes, your **Engage** might be a provocative question instead of a story. Sometimes, **Persuade** might use analogy rather than data. Sometimes, **Inspire** might paint a picture of avoided pain rather than achieved pleasure. Sometimes, **Close** might offer reflection rather than action.

The key is understanding the *purpose* of each element, not just its common expressions.

Practice this: Take one successful message you've created and rewrite it five different ways, maintaining the EPIC structure but varying the tactics within each element. Notice how different approaches serve different audiences and contexts.

The Scaling Secret: Systems Thinking

Here's what most people miss about automatic EPIC: it goes beyond making individual messages easier to create. It's about developing systems thinking that transforms entire communication ecosystems.

Consider how a consulting firm owner might apply this systems approach once EPIC becomes automatic. Rather than simply improving individual presentations, they could redesign their entire client journey:

• **Discovery calls** naturally follow EPIC structure, making prospects more likely to engage with the process.

• **Proposals** tell stories that make logical recommendations feel emotionally compelling.

• **Project kickoffs** inspire teams by connecting daily tasks to meaningful outcomes.

• **Progress reports** engage stakeholders with stories of transformation rather than routine status updates.

• **Final presentations** close with clear next steps that clients actually implement.

In this scenario, the close rate might increase significantly, but more importantly, client satisfaction would soar because every touchpoint reinforces their decision to work with the firm.

This is the real power of automatic EPIC. It becomes your default operating system for all professional communication, creating compound effects that extend far beyond individual pieces of content.

When Instinct Meets Strategy

Advanced EPIC practitioners develop what we might call "strategic intuition," the ability to sense not just what message to craft, but when, where, and how to deliver it for maximum impact.

They recognize when their audience needs more **Engage** (struggling with attention) versus more **Persuade** (questioning credibility) versus more **Inspire** (lacking motivation) versus more **Close** (ready to act but unclear how).

They adapt their approach based on context:

• **High-stakes presentations** might require a more deliberate structure.

• **Casual conversations** might emphasize storytelling over closing.

• **Written content** might need more explicit persuasion than verbal communication.

• **Repeat audiences** might respond to callbacks and inside references.

This strategic intuition develops through what expertise researchers call "domain knowledge," deep understanding not just of the framework, but of how it interacts with human psychology, group dynamics, cultural contexts, and situational factors.

The Mastery Paradox

Here's something counterintuitive: the better you become at EPIC, the less you think about EPIC. Masters don't consciously run through the framework; they inhabit it.

This creates what experts term the "mastery paradox." The very thing that makes experts excellent (unconscious competence) can make them poor teachers if they can't remember what it was like to struggle with the basics.

The solution is maintaining what Zen Buddhism calls "beginner's mind," approaching your craft with curiosity and openness, even as your skills advance. Some practical ways to do this:

• **Regularly teach EPIC to others**, forcing you to break down your intuitive process.

• **Experiment with new formats and contexts**, pushing yourself back into conscious learning.

• **Study other communication frameworks**, comparing approaches and identifying synthesis opportunities.

• **Seek feedback from diverse audiences**, staying calibrated to different perspectives.

The Technology Accelerator

The **EPIC Impact™** App represents a breakthrough in accelerating the journey from conscious competence to unconscious excellence. Rather than replacing human judgment, it amplifies pattern recognition and provides real-time feedback during the learning process.

The app's AI analyzes your content for EPIC elements, suggesting improvements and identifying opportunities. But more importantly, it helps you recognize patterns in your own communication style, accelerating the development of strategic intuition.

Think of it as having a communication coach available 24/7, one that learns your voice while helping you strengthen your structure. The technology doesn't create automatic expertise, but it can significantly compress the timeline for developing it.

Your Path to Automaticity

The journey from framework to instinct isn't mysterious, but it does require intentional practice. Here's your roadmap:

Weeks 1-4: Foundation Building

• Apply EPIC consciously to every significant communication.

• Focus on getting the basic structure right before optimizing.

• Collect examples of effective messages from others.

Weeks 5-8: Pattern Recognition

• Start noticing EPIC elements in the media you consume.

• Practice rapid message structuring (set a timer for 5 minutes).

• Experiment with different tactics within each element.

Weeks 9-12: Emotional Calibration

• Pay attention to audience response and adjust accordingly.

• Practice reading the room during presentations.

• Seek feedback on message effectiveness.

Weeks 13-16: Flexibility Development

• Intentionally break the "rules" while maintaining the principles.

• Adapt EPIC for different contexts and audiences.

• Begin teaching others the framework.

Weeks 17-20: Strategic Integration

• Apply EPIC thinking to communication systems, not just individual messages.

- Develop signature approaches that reflect your unique voice.

- Start innovating within the framework.

Ongoing: Mastery Maintenance

- Continue learning and experimenting.

- Teach others to maintain a beginner's mind.

- Contribute to the evolution of the framework.

The Automaticity Dividend

When EPIC becomes automatic, you unlock what we call the "automaticity dividend," benefits that compound over time.

Creative Freedom: Your conscious mind is freed from structural concerns, allowing deeper creative exploration within proven patterns.

Stress Reduction: Knowing you can handle any communication challenge reduces anxiety and imposter syndrome.

Opportunity Recognition: You begin seeing potential messages and teaching moments everywhere.

Influence Multiplication: Your improved communication naturally makes others want to amplify your message.

Time Leverage: What once took hours now takes minutes, allowing you to create more content or invest time in other priorities.

Authentic Authority: People sense your communication competence, even if they can't articulate why your messages feel different.

The goal isn't to become a communication robot that mechanically applies formulas. The goal is to develop such fluency with effective communication principles that you can focus entirely on serving your audience's needs rather than worrying about your own performance.

When that happens, something magical occurs: your authentic voice becomes inseparable from effective structure. You don't have to choose between being yourself and being strategic. The framework becomes the vehicle through which your unique perspective reaches the world with maximum impact.

That's when you know EPIC has become automatic. And that's when your real influence begins.

This book is the 'why' and the resources are the 'strategy.'

—

In our next chapter, we'll explore how AI amplifies this automatic expertise, scaling your voice without sacrificing authenticity...

i

PART 3: FROM FRAMEWORK TO FORCE AND THE EPIC IMPACT™ APP

YOUR MESSAGE IS MORE THAN CONTENT. IT'S A MOVEMENT IN MOTION.

CHAPTER 11: WHY AI NEEDS THE HUMAN HEART

SCALE YOUR VOICE WITHOUT LOSING YOUR AUTHENTICITY.

You've mastered the **EPIC Framework™**. You've seen how it transforms messaging across industries. Now comes the question that keeps most communicators stuck. "How do I create this level of messaging consistently without burning out?"

The answer isn't working harder. It's working smarter with AI as your creative partner.

But here's what most people get wrong about AI. They assume it's supposed to replace their voice. The truth? The best AI-generated content sounds exactly like you, just faster, more consistent, and infinitely scalable.

The Great AI Awakening That Almost Wasn't

I was hesitant to give AI a try. I didn't have any strong opinion against it; I just had not experienced the transformation that I was soon to discover.

A colleague and I teamed up to host a workshop for local business leaders. I thought I was just there to teach marketing. I had no idea I was about to get schooled by a participant named Emil.

Right before my presentation started, Emil raised his hand and asked, "Would it be okay if my AI app recorded this session?"

"Sure," I said, thinking it was just a fancy way to take notes. Little did I know, Emil wasn't just recording. His app was analyzing, summarizing, organizing, and even distinguishing between the voices of all 20 participants in the room.

I was gobsmacked! And then Emil casually dropped the real bombshell: "Oh, AI can also help you automate tasks, create strategic plans, and save hours every day."

Cue my jaw hitting the floor.

As someone who lives for efficiency (if efficiency were an Olympic sport, I'd have a gold medal), I couldn't believe what I was seeing. This wasn't just helpful. It was life-changing. I went home, started exploring AI, and couldn't sleep for three nights.

My brain raced with ideas about how this tool could simplify my workload, help me make smarter decisions, free up time for high-impact projects, and most importantly, create strategies to scale my messaging without losing my authentic voice.

That sleepless weekend changed everything. Not just for me, but for every client I work with now.

The 30,000-Word Breakthrough

Let me show you exactly what I mean. A few months ago, I sat down with Dr. Marion Platt, the executive director of Star Gospel Mission in Charleston. What started as a simple interview that was supposed to be 45 minutes turned into an incredible three-and-a-half-hour conversation about hope, transformation, and second chances.

When it was over, I had a 30,000-word raw audio transcript. That's 60 pages of single-spaced content. More words than most people write in a year. The old me would have spent weeks trying to turn this into usable content, if I even attempted it at all.

Instead, I decided to let AI do what it does best. Organize, structure, and multiply.

From that one conversation, I created multiple pieces of content:

• A categorized list of all topics discussed for future reference

• A polished article about nonprofit leadership

• A four-part email sequence about transformation stories

• Three blog posts about community impact

• Two social media posts with hashtags

• A powerful EPIC Intro that captured the entire mission

All in less than an hour.

But here's the part that would have taken me days to figure out manually. **AI helped me identify the golden threads that connected everything**. Dr. Platt's stories about men who went from addiction and homelessness to sobriety and restored family relationships became the backbone of content that could serve multiple purposes across multiple platforms.

The complete transformation process and detailed breakdown of this success story are available in the **EPIC Impact™ Starter Kit,** along with a 5-minute demo showing exactly how I turned our three-hour conversation into weeks of compelling content.

The Bootcamp That Proved Everything

That Star Gospel Mission breakthrough became the foundation for something I never expected my AI Marketing Bootcamp. What started as a way to share these techniques with a few clients has become a four-week intensive that's transforming how leaders create content.

And you know what amazes me? My students are mastering these techniques with just two hours per week for four weeks. That's it. Eight total hours to go from AI-intimidated to AI-Mavericks.

Take Mandy Spence from Aura Aesthetics. She started "not even knowing how to log in to ChatGPT." Four weeks later? She's creating blog outlines, Instagram content, and full email sequences. As she put it, "Turning one blog into a month of content? Total game-changer."

Or Sarah Panus, who came in "barely using AI" and left with multiple custom GPTs for her business, podcast, and motherhood. Her Story Library now automatically pulls her experiences into emails, completely changing how she writes.

Eight hours. Four weeks. Complete transformation. It doesn't take long to grasp the incredible opportunity available, and then it can completely transform your everyday tasks. From content ideas to creation to strategic planning. I think it's the best invention of my lifetime!

The Voice Amplification System

What my bootcamp students learn and what the Star Gospel Mission experience taught me is that AI isn't about replacing your personality. It's about amplifying it at scale. Instead of staring at blank pages, second-guessing every word, and editing yourself into generic medi-ocrity, you become the director of your own content creation process.

The system works in three phases. Let's start with the foundation that makes everything else possible.

Phase 1: Voice Capture - Teaching AI to Sound Like You

Before AI can amplify your voice, it needs to master your voice. Most people skip this step and wonder why their AI-generated content sounds robotic. You're going to do it right.

This is exactly what we cover in Week 1 of my "Master AI for Marketing Messaging" bootcamp. We clarify your brand voice and craft messages that truly resonate with your audience.

The foundational approach involves what I call "Voice DNA Extraction." You provide AI with examples of your best writing, and it learns to identify your unique patterns like your sentence structure, word choices, storytelling approach, and the emotions you evoke in readers.

Step 1: Voice DNA Extraction You provide AI with examples of your best writing, and it learns to identify your unique patterns such as your sentence structure, word choices, storytelling approach, and the emotions you evoke in readers.

Step 2: Build Your Authority Bank Your Authority Bank is your professional wisdom library. Here's how to create it and what to include:

• **Signature Stories:** 3-5 client transformations or personal experiences you reference often

• **Core Frameworks:** Your proven methods, processes, or concepts (the "how-to" of your expertise)

• **Industry Insights:** Your unique perspective on trends, challenges, or opportunities in your field

• **Transformation Outcomes:** Specific results your work creates for clients or audiences

How to Organize It:

• Create one document for each category above

• Write each item as if explaining to a colleague

• Include context such as when you use it, why it works, what results it creates

• Keep entries concise but complete (2-3 paragraphs each)

Think of it as giving AI access to your professional wisdom and experience in an organized, accessible way.

The combination of your Voice DNA and Authority Bank creates the foundation for authentic, scalable content creation that sounds exactly like you. The specific prompts and step-by-step process for building these assets are detailed in the **EPIC Impact™** App.

Phase 2: Content Multiplication - From One Idea to Many Formats

Once AI understands your voice and has access to your expertise, it's time to multiply your content across platforms and formats. This is where the magic really happens.

The key is learning to think in content ecosystems rather than individual pieces. A single story, framework, or insight can become a blog post, email sequence, social media content, presentation slides, and video scripts. AI helps you adapt your core message to different audiences, platforms, and purposes while maintaining your authentic voice throughout.

This phase teaches you to see connections between ideas and transform one conversation or experience into weeks of valuable content. The systematic approach to content multiplication ensures you're never starting from scratch again.

Phase 3: Strategic Automation - Building Your Content Engine

The final phase moves beyond individual content creation to building sustainable systems. This is where you create what I call your "Content Engine" - a streamlined process that turns your ongoing experiences, conversations, and insights into a steady flow of engaging content.

You'll learn to identify the types of content that resonate most with your audience, establish content themes that align with your business goals, and create workflows that make content creation feel effortless rather than overwhelming. The goal isn't to replace human creativity but to amplify it.

This phase transforms content creation from a time-consuming task into a strategic advantage that grows your influence and impact without burning you out.

Where This All Leads

Mastering AI-enhanced storytelling isn't just about creating content faster. It's about achieving something unprecedented: the ability to maintain genuine human connection while reaching more people than ever before.

The **EPIC Framework™** provides the structure. AI provides the scale. Your authentic voice provides the heart.

Together, they transform how you communicate, influence, and create impact. No more staring at blank pages. No more wondering if your message will resonate. No more choosing between authenticity and efficiency.

Your message deserves to be heard. The tools exist to make it happen. The question isn't whether you should embrace this technology. The question is: are you ready to amplify your authentic voice and create the impact you've always envisioned?

The foundational templates and implementation strategies for AI-enhanced EPIC messaging are available in the **EPIC Impact™ Starter Kit** at **epicimpact.com**

—

Coming up next: the advanced storytelling moves that will take your messaging to the next level and help you master the art of influence through story.

i

CHAPTER 12: EPIC STORYTELLING MOVES

ADVANCED TECHNIQUES THAT BEND TIME, BUILD TRUST, AND INSPIRE BELIEF.

Once you've mastered the basic **EPIC Framework™**, you can elevate your storytelling even further by mastering five cinematic techniques that captivate audiences and inspire action. I call these "EPIC Storytelling Moves"—powerful ways to manipulate time in your narrative so you drive real results.

The Five Cinematic Techniques That Transform Stories

1 Start at the climax: Begin your story at its most emotional or dramatic point, then explain how you got there. Hook attention and create curiosity.

2 Freeze a moment to build tension: Pause at a critical moment to describe details, emotions, and stakes. Build anticipation before revealing what happens next.

3 Flash back to create empathy: After establishing a current situation, jump backward to show the journey that led to it. Create deeper connection with the person in your story.

4 Compress time to highlight transformation: Skip forward to emphasize the dramatic before-and-after contrasts that showcase your impact.

5 Loop back to tie it all together: End by returning to your opening scene, now enriched with new meaning and emotional resonance.

See the Difference: Standard vs. Enhanced EPIC

Here's a standard EPIC structure for a nonprofit appeal:

Standard Version: "Last Tuesday at 2:17 PM, our shelter reached capacity. Maria, a single mother of three who had fled domestic violence, stood at our front desk with garbage bags of belongings and nowhere to go..."

See how the five cinematic techniques transform the same story:

Enhanced with Storytelling Moves: "Maria sobbed as she placed her children's backpacks by the shelter door. 'We have to leave now?' her 7-year-old asked. 'But I have school tomorrow.' Before our intake coordinator could answer, the phone rang. It was another shelter with space. Just not for all three children together."

See how bending time creates a more dynamic, emotionally resonant story while still following the **EPIC Framework™?** The time manipulation techniques add layers of emotion and urgency without sacrificing authenticity or clarity.

Why These Techniques Work: The Science Behind the Story

These storytelling moves aren't just creative flourishes. They're based on how the human brain processes and remembers information:

Peak-End Rule: People primarily remember the most intense moment (the peak) and the ending of an experience. By starting at the climax and looping back at the end, you're strategically placing your message at the two points most likely to be remembered.

Narrative Transportation: When people are "transported" into a story, they become less critical and more emotionally engaged. Time-bending techniques increase this transportation effect.

Emotional Contrast: Our brains are wired to notice change. By compressing time to show before/after transformations, you create emotional contrast that makes your impact more visceral and compelling.

Strategic Application: When to Use Each Technique

These storytelling moves are powerful, but they should be deployed strategically. Each technique serves specific purposes and works best in particular situations.

The **EPIC Impact™ Starter Kit** offers detailed guidance on when and how to use each technique, along with templates that help you identify the perfect moments in your stories to apply these advanced moves.

From Good to Unforgettable

These storytelling techniques don't replace the **EPIC Framework™**. They enhance it. They work within the structure to create stories that feel more dynamic, emotional, and memorable.

When you bend time in your storytelling, you do more than boost engagement. You inspire meaningful action that transforms lives.

Master These Moves with Interactive Tools

Ready to practice these advanced techniques? The **EPIC Impact™** App provides:

• **Interactive story builders** that guide you through applying each cinematic technique

• **Before-and-after examples** showing how the same story transforms with these moves

• **AI-powered suggestions** for identifying the best moments in your stories to apply time-bending techniques

• **Templates for each technique** that you can customize for your specific industry and audience

• **Practice scenarios** with immediate feedback on your story-telling choices

The app transforms these advanced concepts from theory into practical skills you can apply immediately to your messaging, fundraising appeals, sales conversations, and leadership communications.

Access the **EPIC Impact™** App at **epicimpact.ai** and discover how cinematic storytelling can elevate every message you share.

AI-Powered Storytelling!

—

Coming up next: What if your most powerful stories could multiply themselves? What if the people you serve became your most authentic advocates, sharing their own EPIC stories in ways that create exponential impact? Discover the strategic approach that transforms program participants into powerful messengers.

i

CHAPTER 13: THE MULTIPLIER EFFECT: HOW ONE MESSAGE CREATES MANY MESSENGERS

THE EPIC STRATEGY THAT TRANSFORMS PROGRAM PARTICIPANTS INTO POWERFUL ADVOCATES

Three months ago, I never imagined leading a storytelling workshop with six fathers. Men shaped by trauma, addiction, incarceration, and loss.

I didn't see myself as qualified.

But now I understand: my story was preparing me for that moment.

A Wound I Never Saw Coming

On the last day of kindergarten in South Florida, Karriem Edwards lost his father to a heroin overdose.

Decades later, in upstate South Carolina, my two sons watched their father succumb to meth addiction and serve two years in prison.

Different cities, decades apart. Different circumstances. Same ache. Same unanswered questions.

As their mom, it broke my heart to see the damage that had been done. And yet, all I could do was hold on to hope that someday, healing would reach all of us.

That pain nearly broke us. But what saved us, what healed us, was the power of rewriting our story.

Thankfully, in time, my sons' father overcame his addiction and began to restore his relationship with them. But the a deep wound in their hearts might never have healed if he hadn't been willing to bridge the gap.

From Brokenness to Breakthrough

I had the honor of partnering with the South Carolina Center for Fathers and Families, led by Karriem Edwards. A man who turned his deepest wound into a mission to restore and rebuild fatherhood across the state.

I introduced his Father Fellows, a group of men navigating reentry, redemption, and reconnection, to the **EPIC Framework™** combined with therapeutic storytelling principles that help individuals turn pain into purpose.

"It was therapeutic... I actually didn't even have to go to therapy. It opened up a lot of everything, a lot of things I needed to say. I was around the right people to say it to," said, William, Father Fellow

---

The Ultimate Program ROI: When Beneficiaries Become Your Best Advocates

Three weeks after our EPIC storytelling workshop with the South Carolina Center for Fathers and Families, I found myself on a follow-up virtual call that would forever change how I think about program impact. What I witnessed wasn't just transformation. It was multiplication.

Nicholas and James had already been interviewed on local TV stations. William was preparing for another media appearance. Pierre was gearing up to speak at a grand opening. And most remarkably, they were all still talking about the workshop, not as a one-time event, but as an ongoing catalyst for their personal and professional growth.

This is the hidden power of EPIC: it doesn't just help participants tell their stories. It transforms them into confident ambassadors who can authentically represent your program's impact to the world.

Why Beneficiaries Make the Most Powerful Advocates

Authenticity Resonates: When Nicholas sat down for his Fox TV interview, he didn't need talking points from the communications team. He had his own story, refined through EPIC, that naturally wove in the program's impact. As Dr. Ford noted, *"I could tell he practiced. He had written something out... He was spot on."*

—Dr. Lawrence E. Ford, Sr., D.Min. Director of Marketing and Communications, SC Center for Fathers and Families

Lived Experience Trumps Marketing: No marketing campaign can match the credibility of someone who has actually walked the journey. When William spoke about going from "ATM dad" to emotionally present father, his words carried weight that no organizational brochure could match.

Ripple Effect of Inspiration: Each Father Fellow who shares their story doesn't just promote the program; they also give hope to other fathers who see themselves on the same journey. Pierre captured this perfectly: "I'm hoping I get more opportunities to speak for the Fatherhood Coalition because they have helped me so much."

The EPIC Training Process: Beyond Basic Storytelling

The transformation process follows a strategic approach designed to turn participants into confident, authentic advocates:

Phase 1: Heart-Centered Foundation - Create psychological safety where participants can explore their stories without judgment.

Phase 2: Story Architecture - Use EPIC's structured approach to help participants identify their core transformation moment, articulate challenges without dwelling in victim mentality, connect personal growth to program impact, and craft messages that stick.

Phase 3: Delivery Training - Equip participants with concise speaker outlines, flexible talking points for different audiences, confidence-building techniques, and media-ready messaging.

The Three-Week Follow-Up: Proof of Lasting Impact

Therapeutic Transformation: The workshop's therapeutic value surprised everyone. *"It was healing for me,"* William said. *"Everything just clicked. Everything was just wonderful."* This emotional release created advocates who spoke from genuine gratitude, not obligation.

Practical Application: Three weeks later, the participants were still actively using the tools. William was updating his resume using techniques learned in the workshop. Pierre was refining his story for upcoming speaking engagements. Both were requesting additional support for specific communication needs.

Organic Multiplication: Without any formal requirements, the participants voluntarily sought speaking opportunities. The participants had become proactive ambassadors, not passive beneficiaries.

The Technology Advantage: Making Every Participant Media-Ready

One of the breakthrough elements of our approach was incorporating AI-enhanced storytelling tools, which removed common barriers to effective communication.

Pierre's reflection revealed a universal challenge: *"I will talk and talk and ramble and ramble... The AI really helped pull it together into a cohesive story."* By addressing this struggle, we made confident communication accessible to everyone.

The **EPIC Impact™** app's AI capabilities equipped us to create personalized speaker outlines, multiple versions of their story (30-second, 2-minute, 10-minute formats), video scripts tailored to specific audiences, and professional bios for media appearances.

As Karriem observed, *"Nicholas didn't know what the interview was going to be about. But he had stuff on his phone, and I could tell he had practiced. He understood what he was going to talk about."*

The Multiplication Effect: Measuring True ROI

Within weeks of the workshop, the results spoke for themselves:

Media Amplification: Two participants appeared on television, multiple speaking engagements were booked, social media content was being created organically, and word-of-mouth referrals increased.

Program Credibility: When potential participants hear from someone who has lived the experience, enrollment barriers dissolve. These ambassadors provide social proof that no marketing budget can buy.

Staff Efficiency: As Karriem noted: *"All we have to do is stay out of the way."* When participants can articulate program value themselves, staff can focus on service delivery rather than constant advocacy.

Creating Your Ambassador Development Program

The process of transforming participants into powerful advocates follows proven principles that any organization can implement:

Step 1: Identify Natural Storytellers - Look for participants with compelling transformation stories, enthusiasm for the program, basic communication skills, and willingness to share their stories publicly.

Step 2: Invest in Quality Training - Provide professional facilitation, structured frameworks like EPIC, technology tools for ongoing refinement, and follow-up support and coaching.

Step 3: Create Ongoing Opportunities - Maintain a speakers' bureau, provide regular speaking opportunities, create content creation partnerships, and offer advanced training for top performers.

Step 4: Support and Recognize - Provide ongoing coaching, celebrate contributions publicly, offer professional development opportunities, and create pathways for increased involvement.

7 Questions That Turn Participants Into Powerful Storytellers

The transformation you witnessed with the Father Fellows didn't happen by accident. It started with asking the right questions—questions that help participants uncover their most compelling transformation moments.

Whether you're working with program graduates, scholarship recipients, or community members, these seven questions will help you gather authentic, emotional testimonials that highlight real change:

1. Tell me about the challenges you were facing before connecting with us.

• What did a typical day look like back then?

• Describe the emotions you were experiencing at that time.

2. How were those challenges affecting your daily life or mindset?

• Describe a specific moment when you realized these challenges were holding you back.

• Tell me about how that moment felt.

3. What positive changes have you experienced since receiving our support/services?

• Tell me about a moment when you realized things were beginning to shift for the better.

4. How do you feel now, compared to when you started?

• What would you tell someone who's in the same situation you were in when you first came to us?

5. What stood out to you about your experience with us?

• Tell me about a specific person, conversation, or moment that left a lasting impression and why it mattered to you.

6. What would you say to someone considering working with or seeking help from us?

7. How do you feel about us sharing your story?

• Your experience could inspire and encourage others. Tell me about your thoughts on having your story shared in our materials.

Customizing These Questions for Your Organization

These questions are designed to be adaptable. In your **EPIC Impact™ Starter Kit**, you'll find detailed instructions on how to prompt AI to modify these questions to fit your specific organization, audience, and outcomes. Whether you serve veterans, students, healthcare patients, or any other community, the framework remains the same—only the context changes.

Tips for Collecting Powerful Stories:

• **Focus on specific moments:** Ask for real events, memories, or turning points that bring their story to life.

• **Encourage descriptive details:** Help them paint a picture of their experience.

• **Guide genuine emotion:** Support them in reflecting on how they felt before, during, and after the transformation.

• **Connect to future impact:** Let their story inspire the next person who's considering your program.

The Unexpected Benefits

Beyond the obvious advocacy outcomes, organizations discover additional value at both individual and organizational levels:

Individual Benefits:

• **Personal Healing:** The therapeutic value of structured storytelling often exceeds expectations. Participants process their experiences while building advocacy skills.

• **Professional Development:** Skills learned in ambassador training transfer to job interviews, workplace presentations, and personal relationships.

Organizational Benefits:

• **Community Building:** Shared vulnerability creates stronger bonds among participants. As Karriem observed: *"You guys began to bond... it was all totally subliminal, and everybody did it on natural response."*

• **Organizational Culture:** When beneficiaries become advocates, it creates a culture of gratitude and excellence that permeates the entire organization.

The Bottom Line: Investment That Multiplies

The South Carolina Center for Fathers and Families invested one day in **EPIC** training. Three weeks later, they had multiple media appearances generating positive coverage, participants proactively seeking additional speaking opportunities, organic word-of-mouth marketing from credible voices, and increased program credibility and community support.

"As William put it when describing how he now uses the EPIC framework in all areas of his life: 'I just go home and do different things with it. I'm excited.'"

When you transform beneficiaries into ambassadors, you don't just change their lives. You multiply your impact exponentially. Every story they tell, every interview they give, every person they inspire becomes part of your organization's legacy.

That's the true power of EPIC: it turns your greatest success stories into your most powerful advocates, creating a cycle of impact that extends far beyond any single program or participant.

We're developing the **EPIC Impact™** app to include templates, training guides, and AI-powered tools specifically designed to help organizations develop their own ambassador programs. From initial participant identification to ongoing support systems, this technology will make the multiplication effect accessible to any organization ready to amplify their impact through authentic storytelling.

"When fathers thrive, families flourish. And when families flourish, communities rise." - Karriem Edwards, President, South Carolina Center for Fathers and Families

---

—

Coming up next: Discover where storytelling technology is headed and how the **EPIC Impact™** app is making powerful communication accessible to everyone, regardless of their starting point or technical expertise.

i

CHAPTER 14: THE FUTURE OF STORYTELLING WITH AI

WHERE WE GO FROM HERE AND HOW THE EPIC IMPACT™ APP BRINGS IT TO LIFE.

The room held 60 nonprofit leaders, and I could feel the skepticism in the air. Another workshop. Another consultant. Another promise that "this time will be different."

Lakesha McCutchen from Spartanburg County Foundation had organized this training because she was "desperately searching for the right consultant" who could equip their local nonprofits with real storytelling skills. Their challenge was daunting: No staff. No time. No budget.

I asked for a volunteer.

Larry raised his hand. As we talked, he shared the story that changed everything—how his 14-year-old son Christopher took his own life on January 22, 2019. Christopher was funny and handsome, and and when he smiled, it lit up the room. Larry and his wife Cathy made a commitment just days after their loss to do everything in their power to ensure no family would go through what they had experienced.

I had prepared 20 questions that anyone could use to capture their story. Larry simply wrote his answers right below each question—

nothing fancy, just honest responses about Christopher's Hope Foundation and their mission to bring Hope Squad peer intervention programs to South Carolina schools.

During the demo, I took screenshots of Larry's three pages of answers and ran them through the **EPIC Framework™**. Then I read his transformed story aloud to the group.

The room went silent. Here was Larry's raw grief transformed into powerful purpose—how they became the first to bring Hope Squad to the Southeast, how they've now sponsored 26 schools across three counties. The transformation took minutes, not months. Everyone could see how simple it could be.

"There was one specific moment during the workshop when I knew this training would make a real difference," Lakesha later reflected. " When Hailey showed them how she rewrote Larry's story and brought it to life, you could see the lightbulb moments happening around the room. It really showed them that effective storytelling is as simple as 1, 2, 3."

This is the future we're building toward. Not a world where AI replaces human connection, but one where technology makes powerful communication accessible to anyone with a mission worth sharing.

The Revolution That's Already Here

As Lakesha explained, "Many of our nonprofit partners were requesting more training in marketing and communications, yet most didn't have dedicated staff for these critical functions." The breaking point came when "nonprofit leaders kept telling us they didn't realize how many powerful stories they already had in their arsenal."

The **EPIC Framework™** provides the structure that makes storytelling "as simple as 1, 2, 3." But when combined with AI technology, something extraordinary happens: the tools that once required years of communications training become accessible to anyone willing to learn.

What We Learned from Sixty Skeptics

The Spartanburg workshop taught us something crucial about the future of storytelling technology. It's not enough to have powerful tools. People need to believe the tools are actually designed for them.

"After Hailey's Storytelling + AI training," Lakesha observed, "I believe our nonprofits will feel genuinely equipped to craft and tailor stories for diverse audiences. More importantly, they now see AI as a resource that makes marketing and communications actually doable rather than impossible."

This mindset shift from "impossible" to "doable" is the bridge between where communication technology exists today and where it's headed tomorrow. The **EPIC Impact™** app is being built on this foundation: making advanced storytelling techniques not just accessible, but genuinely usable for people who never thought they were "good at this stuff."

Beyond Generic AI: The EPIC Impact™ Difference

While the market floods with generic AI writing tools, we're developing something different. The **EPIC Impact™** app isn't designed to write for you. It's designed to help you discover your most powerful voice and scale it without losing what makes you uniquely you.

Framework-Driven Intelligence

Most AI tools understand language. The **EPIC Impact™** app understands the **EPIC Framework™**. It knows the difference between an engagement hook and an inspiration moment. It recognizes when your story needs more emotional resonance or clearer problem definition. It guides you through each component with the intelligence of a master storyteller and the patience of your most supportive coach.

Industry-Specific Adaptation

Whether you're a nonprofit seeking donor support, a healthcare provider building patient trust, a consultant establishing authority, or an entrepreneur inspiring investment, the app understands your unique communication challenges. It doesn't give you generic templates. It helps you apply EPIC principles to your specific context, audience, and goals.

Voice Clarification, Not Replacement

The Spartanburg participants didn't need AI to think for them. They needed AI to help them think more clearly about what they already knew. The app learns your unique communication style, your values, your perspective, and helps you express your authentic voice with greater clarity and impact.

Real Impact, Real Results

What struck Lakesha most about our work together was the practical outcome: "**EFFICIENCY!!!** That's what this training delivered. Our nonprofits now have practical tools to attract more participants, volunteers, supporters, and funders through better storytelling. They're not just hoping their stories will connect–they know how to make them connect."

This efficiency multiplies when AI enhancement enters the picture. The same nonprofit leader who struggled to write one compelling story can now create multiple versions for different audiences, adapt their message for various platforms, and maintain consistent quality across all their communications.

But here's what makes this sustainable is, they're not dependent on the consultant who taught them. The **EPIC Impact™** app becomes their ongoing coach, helping them improve with every story they tell.

The Technology Behind the Transformation

Story Architecture Intelligence

Behind every great story is intentional structure. The app recognizes story elements you might miss: tension points that need more development, transformation moments that could be more vivid, and connection opportunities that strengthen audience engagement. It's like having a master editor who never gets tired and always sees the potential in your message.

Real-Time Guidance

As you work through your story, the app provides suggestions for enhancing your message using EPIC principles. Too much background information in your engagement section? It notices. Missing emotional resonance in your inspiration? It guides you toward more powerful language. Weak call-to-action? It helps you create urgency without manipulation.

Adaptive Learning

The more you use the app, the better it understands your style, your audience, and your goals. It learns from your successes and helps you replicate what works while avoiding what doesn't.

The Ethics of Influence

As AI makes persuasive communication more accessible, we must anchor our approach in ethics and authenticity. The **EPIC Framework™** was designed with this principle at its core: influence without manipulation.

Lakesha noted what drew her to our approach: "What struck us most about working with Hailey was her genuine passion for giving nonprofits the tools they need to succeed and reach the next level in telling their impact stories. It was never about making money – it was all about helping the nonprofits."

The **EPIC Impact™** app extends this commitment. It won't help you exaggerate outcomes you haven't achieved or promise results you can't deliver. Instead, it helps you discover the most effective way to share what's genuinely true about your mission, values, and impact.

Looking Forward: The Storytelling Democratization

Five years from now, we'll look back at this moment as the turning point when storytelling mastery became accessible to everyone. Not just to those born with natural charisma or expensive communications training, but to anyone with a mission worth sharing.

Sixty people who walked in thinking they "weren't good at marketing" walked out with their own polished EPIC introductions and the confidence to use them. When AI enhancement is added to this foundation, the possibilities become limitless.

The EPIC Impact™ App: Your Next Step

We're currently developing the **EPIC Impact™** app based on insights from workshops like the one in Spartanburg. Features include:

Story Builder: Guided creation using the **EPIC Framework™** with AI suggestions tailored to your industry and audience

Voice Training: AI that learns your unique communication style and helps you maintain authenticity while improving clarity and impact

Message Multiplier: Transform one core story into multiple formats for different platforms and purposes

Efficiency Tools: Practical resources that make marketing and communications "doable rather than impossible"

Community Connection: Connect with other EPIC communicators for feedback, collaboration, and continued growth

The app launches with early access for readers of this book. Visit epicimpact.ai to join the waitlist and be among the first to experience the future of ethical, AI-enhanced storytelling.

Beyond This Book: Continuing Your Journey

Mastering the **EPIC Framework™** is just the beginning. Your most powerful stories are often born from your most challenging experiences. If you're ready to dive deeper into turning your personal story into professional impact, my upcoming book ***Rewrite the Story That Tried to Break You—And Turn It Into Strategies That Stick®*** will take you on that journey.

What if the hardest chapter of your life was actually the beginning of your greatest calling?

This book is part memoir, part strategy guide, and all heart. It's for mission-driven leaders, entrepreneurs, and everyday overcomers who've walked through adversity and are now ready to lead with clarity, confidence, and conviction.

Inside, you'll discover:

The REWRITE Framework™ – Reframe your past and reclaim your future with purpose

Advanced EPIC Strategies – Turn your message into a movement that sticks and builds lasting influence

In a world full of noise, numbing, and AI-generated fluff, the most powerful thing you can offer is your truth, told with purpose, resilience, and strategy.

The Story Continues

Lakesha McCutchen and her sixty nonprofit leaders proved something important: when you give people the right framework and the right tools, they don't just learn to tell better stories. They discover they had powerful stories all along.

The **EPIC Framework™** provides the structure. AI provides the acceleration. Your authentic voice provides the heart. Together, they create something unprecedented: the ability for anyone with a mission to master the art of influence.

The world is waiting for leaders who can cut through the noise with clarity, who can inspire action through authentic story, who can build movements that matter. The tools exist. The technology is ready.

Are you ready to create your **EPIC Impact™?**

Your story starts now.

AI-Powered Storytelling!

i

APPENDIX: THE FRAMEWORK FACE-OFF

EPIC VS. STORYBRAND, AIDA, PASTOR, AND THE GOLDEN CIRCLE

EPIC vs. StoryBrand vs. PASTOR vs. AIDA vs. Golden Circle

Understanding Communication Frameworks

In the world of storytelling and communication, different frameworks serve different purposes. Like tools in a craftsperson's workshop, each has been designed to solve specific challenges and achieve particular outcomes. Understanding these differences helps you choose the right approach for your goals.

The five frameworks we'll examine represent the most influential approaches to structured communication today. Each has earned its place through proven results in specific contexts, and each offers unique strengths worth understanding.

The 5 Framework Comparison

Framework	Personal Communication	Business Communication	Marketing Applications	Creative Writing	Public Speaking	Universal Adaptability
EPIC	☑ Excellent - works for all personal interactions	☑ Excellent - adapts to any business context	☑ Excellent - effective across all marketing channels	☑ Excellent - natural story structure	☑ Excellent - complete presentation framework	☑ True Universal
StoryBrand	! Specialized - designed for customer relationships	☑ Excellent - purpose-built for business contexts	☑ Excellent - specifically designed for marketing	! Specialized - customer-hero model has specific use	☑ Good - works well for business presentations	! Business-Focused
PASTOR	☑ Good - effective for problem-solving conversations	☑ Good - strong in coaching/ministry contexts	! Specialized - works best for problem-aware audiences	! Specialized - structured for specific narrative types	☑ Excellent - designed for motivational speaking	! Problem-Solution Focused
AIDA	! Specialized - designed for influence contexts	☑ Good - effective for direct sales contexts	☑ Excellent - classic direct response framework	! Specialized - works for action-driven narratives	☑ Good - effective for persuasive presentations	! Marketing-Focused
Golden Circle	☑ Good - effective for purpose-driven conversations	☑ Excellent - ideal for organizational communication	☑ Good - strong for mission-based marketing	! Specialized - works for theme-driven stories	☑ Excellent - perfect for inspirational speaking	! Purpose-Focused

EPIC: The Universal Communication Framework

EPIC (Engage, Persuade, Inspire, Close) distinguishes itself as the only framework designed to work across every form of human communication. Its power lies in following the natural psychological sequence that drives all meaningful interaction.

Core Philosophy: Every effective communication must engage attention, persuade the mind, inspire the heart, and compel action. This sequence works universally because it mirrors how humans naturally process information and make decisions.

The Four Universal Elements:

Engage - Capture and maintain attention with an emotional hook (essential in every context)

Persuade - Present your story with logical reasoning and build credibility (required for all influence)

Inspire - Create emotional connection by painting a vision and issuing a call to action (drives meaningful action)

Close - Direct specific next steps with clarity and confidence (necessary for any outcome)

Why EPIC Works Everywhere: Unlike specialized frameworks, EPIC addresses the complete psychological journey of communication. Whether you're writing fiction, delivering presentations, holding personal conversations, or creating marketing campaigns, you still need to engage attention with emotion, build acceptance through story, create inspiration through vision, and motivate action with confident next steps.

Each Framework Has Its Strengths

Each framework was created to solve specific communication challenges:

StoryBrand revolutionized business communication by making complex value propositions clear and customer-focused.

PASTOR provides structure for addressing difficult topics while maintaining hope.

AIDA offers a time-tested approach for driving immediate action.

Golden Circle transformed how leaders communicate vision and purpose.

EPIC encompasses elements of all these approaches while working across every communication context. It engages like the best attention-grabbing techniques, persuades like the most logical systems, inspires like the most emotional approaches, and drives action like the most effective call-to-action strategies.

Framework Integration Strategies

Sophisticated communicators often combine frameworks strategically:

For Comprehensive Business Communication:

• EPIC for leadership development and personal growth

• StoryBrand for customer-facing messaging

• AIDA for specific campaign elements

• Golden Circle for organizational foundation

For Personal Development:

• EPIC for overall growth and communication skill building

• PASTOR for addressing specific life challenges

• Golden Circle for clarifying personal purpose and direction

For Content Creation:

• EPIC as the foundational structure for all content

- StoryBrand for business-focused pieces

- AIDA for conversion-oriented materials

- Golden Circle for vision and mission content

The Learning Investment

Each framework requires different levels of commitment to master:

Quick Implementation (1-2 hours):

- **AIDA:** Straightforward formula with clear steps

- **PASTOR:** Structured approach with defined progression

Moderate Investment (1-2 days):

- **StoryBrand:** Requires understanding customer psychology

- **Golden Circle:** Needs deep exploration of purpose and values

Ongoing Development (continuous practice):

- **EPIC:** Involves personal growth alongside communication skill building

Making Your Framework Choice

Consider these factors when selecting your primary framework:

Your Communication Goals

- Single context optimization vs. universal effectiveness

- Immediate results vs. long-term development

• Specialized expertise vs. broad competency

Your Audience Needs

• Specific customer segments vs. diverse audiences

• Problem-aware vs. unaware audiences

• Action-oriented vs. inspiration-seeking audiences

Your Personal Style

• Systematic vs. intuitive approach

• Business-focused vs. holistic development

• Specialized mastery vs. universal application

Your Context Requirements

• Single-use campaigns vs. ongoing communication

• Team consistency vs. individual expression

• Measurable outcomes vs. relationship building

The Universal Truth of Communication

Regardless of which framework you choose, effective communication requires attention, logical acceptance, emotional connection, and behavioral motivation. This sequence occurs whether you're having a personal conversation, delivering a business presentation, creating marketing content, or writing fiction.

EPIC makes this universal sequence explicit and intentional, providing a framework that works across every context you'll encounter. Other frameworks optimize specific aspects of this sequence for particular situations, making them valuable tools for specialized applications.

Conclusion: The Right Framework for Your Mission

Each framework in this comparison has earned its place through proven results in specific contexts. StoryBrand clarifies business messaging and improves customer engagement. PASTOR provides hope alongside problem-solving. AIDA drives immediate action and measurable results. Golden Circle inspires purpose-driven loyalty and organizational alignment.

EPIC stands apart by working effectively across all these contexts while facilitating personal transformation alongside communication development. It's the framework that grows with you, adapting to every situation while building both internal authenticity and external effectiveness.

The foundational templates and implementation strategies for AI-enhanced EPIC messaging are available in the **EPIC Impact™** app at epicimpact.ai.

AI-Powered Storytelling!

The best framework choice depends on your specific goals, audience, and context. For specialized applications, focused frameworks offer optimized solutions. For universal effectiveness and personal development, EPIC provides a comprehensive capability that serves every communication challenge you'll face.

Your communication shapes your relationships, career, and impact on the world. Select the framework that best serves your goals while meeting your audience's needs.

The key lies in understanding what each framework does best, then choosing strategically based on your unique situation and long-term communication goals.

i

YOUR REVIEW CHANGES LIVES. READY TO
TAKE EPIC TO THE NEXT LEVEL?

You did it! You made it through every chapter, every framework, every story that brought us together on this journey. As someone who believes deeply in the power of words to change lives, I can't tell you how much it means to me that you invested your time in these pages.

Your journey with EPIC doesn't end here. It's just beginning. But before you go out and start turning messages into movements, I have a small favor to ask.

Your Words Could Change Another Leader's Life

If this book helped you in any way, whether you discovered a new perspective on storytelling, refined your messaging strategy, or simply felt less alone in your communication struggles, ***would you consider leaving a review?***

Here's the thing: reviews aren't just nice to have. They're how other mission-driven leaders find books that could revolutionize their organizations. Your honest feedback helps the right book find the right person at exactly the right moment. And as a new author, every single review helps me reach more people who need these tools to create real impact. Your encouragement keeps me going on the hard days.

Where to Leave Reviews:

• **Amazon** - Even if you didn't purchase there, you can still review if you have an Amazon account

• **Goodreads** - The world's largest community of readers

• **Barnes & Noble** - Online reviews welcome from all readers

• **Your social media** - Share your biggest takeaway with your network

Even a single sentence, such as *"This framework actually works"* or *"Finally, a storytelling approach that feels authentic,"* can make the difference between someone discovering this book or scrolling past it. Your review doesn't just help future readers—it helps expand this movement.

Gift It Forward

Know a mission-driven leader who could use encouragement? Someone struggling to find their voice or communicate their impact? Pass this book along to them. Sometimes the greatest gift we can give another leader is the reminder that they're just one story away from breakthrough.

Ready to Take EPIC to the Next Level?

If you're thinking, "This is exactly what my team needs," you're not alone. Organizations across the country are revolutionizing their communication using these same principles.

Want to bring EPIC to your organization?

Visit **haileyevans.com** to explore how we can work together:

Workshops & Training - I help leaders turn their stories into tools for impact. In story-driven sessions, teams learn to craft messages that build trust, spark emotion, and inspire support, whether they're fundraising, leading, or growing their audience.

• **Workshops:** Hands-on storytelling skills to boost support

• **Keynotes:** High-impact talks that inspire action

• **The EPIC Impact™ App:** Story-enhanced content, ready in seconds

• **The EPIC Impact™ Community:** Join a supportive network of mission-driven leaders who are transforming their communication and amplifying their impact.

Whether your team needs a half-day workshop, a keynote that energizes your conference, or ongoing support through the **EPIC Impact™** App, there's a solution that fits your needs and budget.

You're Not Just a Reader. You're Part of the Movement

Remember what we learned in Chapter 1? You're just one story away from breakthrough. Now you have the framework to make it happen.

Whether you're leading a nonprofit, running a business, or simply trying to communicate truth more clearly, you now have tools that can change not just your message but your impact.

Go out there and use them. The world needs your voice, your story, and your leadership.

And when you see the results (because you will), I hope you'll share them with me. I love hearing how EPIC changes real organizations and real lives. **You can reach me at hailey@haileyevans.com**

Connect With Me—just search for Hailey Evans.

• Facebook

- LinkedIn

- YouTube

- Instagram

- Amazon Author Page

Thank you for trusting me with your time. Thank you for believing that better communication can create a better world. Now go make some magic happen.

With gratitude and excitement for your journey ahead!

You're just one story away,

Hailey Evans

P.S. - If you're feeling stuck on where to start with EPIC, remember: begin with just one message this week. Pick something you need to send anyway, apply the framework, and watch what happens. Small shifts create big breakthroughs.

AI-Powered Storytelling!

WHAT'S NEXT: YOUR STORY ISN'T OVER

A PREVIEW OF THE UPCOMING BOOK THAT TURNS YOUR HARDEST CHAPTERS INTO STRATEGIES THAT STICK®.

This is just the beginning. I have so much more to share with you, starting with my next book: **Rewrite the Story That Tried to Break You —and *Turn It Into Strategies That Stick®***

We all have a breaking point. Mine didn't come when I found out I was pregnant three weeks before graduating high school at seventeen. It didn't come after my 14-year marriage ended with his shocking confession of 22 affairs, or when I sat in a courthouse signing bankruptcy papers with a toddler on my hip. It didn't even come when I watched my sons' father get handcuffed at their high school soccer game, with parents whispering and teammates staring.

It came on a rainy Tuesday night. I was six weeks into a job I had fought hard to land. After four years on food stamps, working toward my third college degree (earned without a single dollar of debt) and a decade of clawing my way out of survival mode, I finally felt like I was making it.

Until I didn't.

I crashed. Literally. The impact of the crash didn't just break my car. It shattered my momentum. What doctors first called a concussion turned out to be a traumatic brain injury that plunged me into two years of isolation, chronic pain, and deafening silence.

I couldn't watch TV. Couldn't listen to music. I wore sunglasses and earplugs in my own home. I had migraines so severe I had to lie still in a dark room for hours at a time.

But in that dark room, I realized something: my story wasn't over. It just needed a rewrite.

That rewrite became the foundation of everything that followed and the framework you're about to discover. Whether you're starting over after heartbreak, rebuilding after financial loss, raising a family, navigating a career change, or leading a mission-driven organization, this book will guide you back to your story's power.

Because your voice still matters, your purpose is still valid, and your next chapter is waiting.

Stay Connected for What's Coming Next

Follow me as an author on Amazon so you'll know the moment new books are published. I promise there's a lot more coming.

Join my newsletter community at **haileyevans.com** to stay updated on:

• New book releases and early previews

• Exclusive **EPIC Framework™** resources

• Real-world case studies from organizations using these strategies

• Behind-the-scenes stories from my own journey

With gratitude and excitement for your journey ahead!

You're just one story away,

Hailey Evans

BIBLIOGRAPHY AND SOURCES

Chapter 1: One Story Away®

i. Covenant House case study: Covenant House Annual Report (2022), "Donor Engagement Strategy Results"

Chapter 2: Noise Isn't the Enemy, Confusion Is

i. Brown, B. (2018). *Dare to lead: Brave work. Tough conversations. Whole hearts.* New York, NY: Random House.

Miller, D. (2017). *Building a StoryBrand: Clarify your message so customers will listen.* Nashville, TN: HarperCollins Leadership.

Wright, A. (2023). *Transformation Tuesday: A case study in donor communications. Journal of Advancement Communications,* 8(2).

Chapter 3: Clarity is Kindness (and Power)

i. Duffy Health Foundation. (2024). *Annual appeal analysis report.* Internal publication.

Oklahoma Medical Research Foundation. (2024). *Donor response metrics 2021–2024.* Internal report by OMRF Communications Department.

Chapter 4: What Makes a Message Stick?

i. Ahern, T. (2016). *How to write fundraising materials that raise more money.* Emerson & Church Publishers.

Bruner, J. (1986). *Actual minds, possible worlds.* Cambridge, MA: Harvard University Press.

Fiske, S. T., & Taylor, S. E. (1991). *Social cognition* (2nd ed.). New York, NY: McGraw-Hill.

Green, M. C., & Brock, T. C. (2000). The role of transportation in the persuasiveness of public narratives. *Journal of Personality and Social Psychology,* 79(5), 701–721.

Lee, J., & Skadberg, A. (2020). Storytelling and volunteer retention: A field experiment at cultural institutions. *Journal of Arts Management, Law, and Society,* 50(1), 32–44.

Oppenheimer, D. M., & Olivola, C. Y. (Eds.). (2011). *The science of giving: Experimental approaches to the study of charity.* New York, NY: Psychology Press.

Rizzolatti, G., & Craighero, L. (2004). The mirror-neuron system. *Annual Review of Neuroscience, 27,* 169–192.

Sargeant, A., & Shang, J. (2017). *Fundraising principles and practice.* San Francisco, CA: Jossey-Bass.

Zak, P. J. (2013). How stories change the brain. *Greater Good Magazine.* Retrieved from https://greatergood.berkeley.edu/article/item/how_stories_change_brain

Network for Good. (2021). *Digital giving index.* Retrieved from https://www.networkforgood.com

The Donor Voice. (2018). *Story-centered supporter communications: Internal research findings.*

Center on Philanthropy. (2019). *Healthcare fundraising impact report: Storytelling and corporate partnerships.* Internal publication.

Chapter 5: Forget Copywriting. Start Leading

i. Brown, B. (2012). *Daring greatly: How the courage to be vulnerable transforms the way we live, love, parent, and lead.* New York, NY: Avery.

Charity: Water. (2022). *Annual impact report.* Retrieved from https://www.charitywater.org

Darsey, J. (1997). *The prophetic tradition and radical rhetoric in America.* New York, NY: New York University Press.

Feeding America. (2014). *Empty plate campaign results report.* Internal publication.

Fuller, M. (1986). *No more shacks! The daring vision of Habitat for Humanity.* Waco, TX: Word Books.

Harrison, S. (2018). *Thirst: A story of redemption, compassion, and a mission to bring clean water to the world.* New York, NY: Currency.

Khan, S. (2012). *The one world schoolhouse: Education reimagined.* New York, NY: Twelve.

Khan Academy. (2023). *Impact and transparency report.* Retrieved from https://www.khanacademy.org

Nonprofit Marketing Institute. (2024). *State of nonprofit marketing report.* Internal publication.

Sinek, S. (2019). *The infinite game.* New York, NY: Portfolio/Penguin.

Stevenson, B. (2014). *Just mercy: A story of justice and redemption.* New York, NY: Spiegel & Grau.

UNICEF Sweden. (2013). *Likes don't save lives campaign case study.* Retrieved from https://www.unicef.se

UNICEF Sweden. (2013). *Annual report.* Stockholm, SE: UNICEF Sweden.

Chapter 6: Burnout and the Call to Lead Differently

i. Center for Effective Philanthropy. (2024). *State of nonprofits report.* Cambridge, MA: CEP. Retrieved from https://cep.org

Vu Le. (n.d.). *NonprofitAF.* Retrieved from https://nonprofitaf.com

Ronald McDonald House Charities of the Carolinas. (2024). Personal communication and testimonial from Marti Spencer, CEO/Executive Director.

Various mental health statistics referenced in the chapter appear consistent with data from:

Maslach, C., & Leiter, M. P. (2016). *Burnout: A brief history and how to combat it.* Harvard Business Review. Retrieved from https://hbr.org

and

World Health Organization. (2019). *Burn-out an "occupational phenomenon": International classification of diseases.* Retrieved from https://www.who.int

Chapter 7: Enter EPIC: Your Framework for Sustainable Impact

i. Fiske, S. T., & Taylor, S. E. (1991). *Social cognition* (2nd ed.). New York, NY: McGraw-Hill.

Journal of Cognitive Neuroscience. (2023). Neural pathways in problem recognition and solution finding. *Journal of Cognitive Neuroscience, 35*(4), 567–580.

Nelson, Jon. (2024). Personal communication. Association for Christian Fundraising.

Oyserman, D. (2015). Identity-based motivation: Implications for action-readiness, procedural-readiness, and consumer behavior. *Journal of Consumer Psychology, 25*(3), 473–490.

Rizzolatti, G., & Craighero, L. (2004). The mirror-neuron system. *Annual Review of Neuroscience, 27,* 169–192.

Zak, P. J. (2013). How stories change the brain. *Greater Good Magazine.* Retrieved from https://greatergood.berkeley.edu/article/item/how_stories_change_brain

Zak, P. J. (2014). Why your brain loves good storytelling. *Harvard Business Review.* Retrieved from https://hbr.org/2014/10/why-your-brain-loves-good-storytelling

Chapter 8: How Industry Leaders Transform Their Results with One Simple Framework

i. Panus, Sarah. (2024). Personal testimonial. Content Strategist & Host of the *Marketing With Empathy*® Podcast, KindredSpeak.com.

Ramona, Steve. (2024). Personal testimonial. Host of *Doing Business with a Servant's Heart* podcast.

Southeast Land Group Workshop. (2024). Field notes and participant testimonials from Alabama EPIC + AI training session.

Chapter 10: When EPIC Becomes Automatic

i. Angela Duckworth — *deliberate practice* (see *Grit* and related research)

Beginner's mind — a concept from Zen Buddhism encouraging openness and curiosity even at advanced levels of expertise

Chunking — a cognitive psychology and neuroscience term describing how the brain groups information into meaningful units

Domain knowledge — expertise research term describing deep understanding of a specific field

Mastery paradox — the phenomenon where experts, due to unconscious competence, struggle to teach beginners effectively

Mirror neurons — neural mechanism that enables empathy and emotional resonance by mirroring observed behaviors

Perceptual learning — psychological process where repeated exposure sharpens one's ability to discern meaningful patterns

Strategic intuition — concept from decision-making and expertise research describing the ability to act instinctively with strategy

Chapter 11: Why AI Needs the Human Heart

i. Emil — Workshop participant who introduced the author to real-world AI applications.

Mandy Spence — Participant in the AI Marketing Bootcamp from Aura Aesthetics; testimonial shared with permission.

Marion Platt — Executive Director of Star Gospel Mission, Charleston, SC; interview used to demonstrate AI-enhanced storytelling.

Star Gospel Mission — Charleston-based nonprofit featured in a case study on scalable content creation.

Aura Aesthetics — Business featured in a testimonial example of AI-driven content transformation.

Chapter 12: EPIC Storytelling Moves

i. Green, M. C., & Brock, T. C. (2000). The role of transportation in the persuasiveness of public narratives. *Journal of Personality and Social Psychology*, 79(5), 701–721.

Kahneman, D., Fredrickson, B. L., Schreiber, C. A., & Redelmeier, D. A. (1993). When more pain is preferred to less: Adding a better end. *Psychological Science*, 4(6), 401–405.

Chapter 13: The Multiplier Effect: How One Message Creates Many Messengers

i. Edwards, Karriem — President, South Carolina Center for Fathers and Families; shared his personal story and leadership insights featured in the chapter.

Ford, Dr. Lawrence E., Sr., D.Min. — Director of Marketing and Communications, South Carolina Center for Fathers and Families; provided commentary on participant media readiness.

South Carolina Center for Fathers and Families — Nonprofit organization featured in the chapter for its Father Fellows program and ambassador development.

William — Father Fellow participant in the EPIC storytelling workshop; shared his testimony of healing and advocacy.

Nicholas — Father Fellow participant who shared his story in media interviews after the EPIC workshop.

James — Father Fellow participant featured for his advocacy efforts post-workshop.

Pierre — Father Fellow participant highlighted for his speaking engagements and reflections on AI-assisted storytelling.

Chapter 14: The Future of Storytelling with AI

i. Lawrence, Larry — Workshop participant who shared his personal story of loss and founded Christopher's Hope Foundation.

Lawrence, Cathy — Co-founder of Christopher's Hope Foundation, in memory of her son Christopher.

McCutchen, Lakesha — Community Engagement Officer, Spartanburg County Foundation; organized the workshop featured in the chapter and provided reflections.

Spartanburg County Foundation — Nonprofit organization that hosted the nonprofit storytelling + AI training featured in the chapter.

Christopher's Hope Foundation — Nonprofit founded by Larry and Cathy Lawrence in memory of their son, featured as a case study in the chapter.

Hope Squad — Peer intervention program sponsored in South Carolina schools by Christopher's Hope Foundation.

APPENDIX: The Framework Face-Off

i. AIDA — Classic direct-response communication framework (Attention, Interest, Desire, Action) designed to drive immediate action.

Golden Circle — Purpose-driven communication framework by Simon Sinek that emphasizes Why, How, and What.

PASTOR — Hope-oriented storytelling framework developed by Ray Edwards for persuasive, problem-solving communication.

StoryBrand — Business communication framework developed by Donald Miller, designed to clarify business messaging through a customer-as-hero narrative.

EPIC — Engage, Persuade, Inspire, Close; universal communication framework introduced in this book, designed to work across personal, business, marketing, creative, and public speaking contexts.